Presented To:

_____

From:

_____

Date:

_____

RE·FORMING
A NEW YOU

RE·FORMING

A NEW YOU A GUIDE FOR REFORMING YOUR HEART, HOME, & HOPE

WAYMAN MING JR.

DESTINY IMAGE® PUBLISHERS, INC.

P.O. Box 310, Shippensburg, PA 17257-0310

"Promoting Inspired Lives"

This book and all other Destiny Image, Revival Press, MercyPlace, Fresh Bread, Destiny Image Fiction, and Treasure House books are available at Christian bookstores and distributors worldwide.

For a U.S. bookstore nearest you, call 1-800-722-6774.

For more information on foreign distributors, call 717-532-3040.

Reach us on the Internet: www.destinyimage.com.

ISBN 13 TP: 978-0-7684-3909-0

ISBN 13 Ebook: 978-0-7684-8954-5

For Worldwide Distribution, Printed in the U.S.A.

1 2 3 4 5 6 7 8 / 14 13 12 11

DEDICATION

For my wife, Kimberly, who is a godly woman and my biggest encourager. For my sons—Spencer and Garrett—who are still behind the curtain, waiting for their appointed time to make an entrance into the world as godly men who will make a worldwide difference. For my daughter, Gracie, who is God's special gift to her daddy and a spiritual re-former to the world.

ACKNOWLEDGMENTS

When authors write books, they sometimes feel like amateur golfers lining up a three-foot putt. They think they will make the putt, but they're not quite sure. They think their book will make a difference, but there is always a question mark at the end of the sentence. If *Re-Forming a New You* somehow impacts you, it was certainly enhanced by the following:

> *To Him who is able to do exceedingly abundantly above all that we ask or think, according to the power that works in us, to Him be glory in the church by Christ Jesus to all generations* (Ephesians 3:20-21).

To Charles and Janice Scott and my Pentecostal Church of God family, who have opened their hearts to my God-given dreams and visions—you have given me room to write outside the margins of the status quo.

To my wife, Kimberly, who has always encouraged me to live for an audience of One. You have always encouraged me to stand up and be counted, whatever the cost.

To my son Spencer, who is wise beyond his years—you have the potential to shake nations with your words and pen. Simply hear God's voice and obey God's voice. Thank you for believing in your lifelong coach.

To my son Garrett, who has more talent in his little finger than I have in my entire body—always serve the Lord with your talent and maintain a teachable spirit. God gives grace and blesses the humble. I love you, Vazu.

To my daughter, Gracie, who is the apple of her daddy's eye— you are my special Pookie. Thank you for your hugs and kisses.

To my dad, who has always prayed that I would be strong in my weaknesses and humble in my successes—you are more than just a dad. You are a confidant, friend, and spiritual father.

To my mother, who lives vicariously through her children and grandchildren—you will never understand how much of an inspiration you are to all of us. You have raised the spiritual bar in our family and set our spiritual sights on becoming just like you when we grow up.

To my brother, Jared, who is one of the finest pastors in America—you are my best friend. Your love for God, life, and ministry inspires us all. I hope to be there for you as you have been there for me.

To my brother, Brian, who is one of the finest worship leaders in America—you too are my best friend. Your ability to dream dreams and push the envelope of faith moves me beyond words.

To my father and mother-in-law, Doyle and Shirley Thomlison—you have always been a cup of cold water in a dry and weary land. Thank you for loving me as a son you never had.

At the end of a movie, there is always a list of credits given to the behind-the-scenes people who helped in the production process. To all those who helped produce this book, you certainly mean more to me than any list of credits could express. Only in

Heaven will you receive the credit you deserve. Thank you so much for helping me sink the three-foot putt.

ENDORSEMENTS

In his book, Wayman Ming Jr. explores God and the order He operates with. He teaches the importance of not wasting your time on this earth but living a life filled with purpose. I believe each day is a precious gift that should not be simply spent but wisely invested. I pray that as you read this book, you will decide to live with purpose and chase after the calling God has for your life.

RON LUCE
President and Founder of Teen Mania Ministries

Re-Forming a New You presents a unique perspective on living an aggressive, world-changing Christian life. My friend Wayman Ming Jr. has packed dynamite material into this small volume. Be warned that this read is not for the faint of heart, but if you are tired of living an average Christian existence and want to live an extraordinary Christian life like Jesus intended, then this book is for you!

BILLY WILSON
Executive Director, International Center for
Spiritual Renewal and Empowered 21

Why do some people seem to experience more of God's favor in their lives? The simple answer is they allow the Holy Spirit to reform their thinking, opinions, and values. In Wayman Ming Jr.'s writings, you will find valuable wisdom, insight, and direction to reform your life in the favor of God. This book will show you how to reform yourself, your family, and your church.

CHARLES C. SCOTT
General Bishop of the Pentecostal Church of God

Wayman Ming Jr. has done serious followers of Jesus a huge favor! He issues a call to take seriously the questions, challenges, and people that are present in the Bible. While some use the Bible as a source for moralistic thinking, Wayman Ming Jr. takes the Bible seriously. He sees the narratives and prescriptions of the text not merely as worthy suggestions but affirms forcefully that God is still at work in transforming ways that matter for eternity. Underlying his writing is the assumption that we can expect God to show up today in exactly the same way He did in biblical narratives. Taking our culture seriously and the Bible authoritatively, in the dynamic relationship of the Word and the Spirit, is the result of Wayman Ming Jr.'s efforts. Do yourself a favor and read this book—it will be a wise decision.

BYRON D. KLAUS
President of Assemblies of God Theological Seminary

CONTENTS

FOREWORD

My covenant friend, Wayman Ming Jr., has written a dangerous book. It is dangerous, first of all, because of its content. It is an honest, compelling assessment of the challenges concerning the condition of today's Church. Not written with any sense of self-righteousness or condescension, it nevertheless deals honestly with the tremendous crisis of genuine biblical, covenantal Christianity, especially in the Western Church. Systematically dealing with the individual, the home, the Church, and culture at large, Wayman calls us to a healthy introspection that leads to decisive, holy action.

This book is also dangerous because of who has written it. Wayman is a man who has proven himself. He is not a self-proclaimed "prophet," standing outside the Church in condescending judgment. Rather, he has proven himself in years of selfless dedication to helping the Bride of Christ make herself ready for her Bridegroom. When you are around Wayman, you have a deep sense that you are around someone who has decided fully, "For me to live is Christ...." This book, which is really a trumpet call from the heart of God, is not written with clinical assessment or critical abstraction; rather, it is the heart of one who is bearing the burden along with us, calling us, in vulnerability and focused intensity, to become much more than we are.

This book is not to be read but experienced. Reading this book from the mind only would be like starting a course of antibiotics and stopping them halfway through the treatment. You would be better off to not begin in the first place. This book should be meditated on with prayerful reverence in the Lord: First, because it accurately describes what we all know but don't want to admit—the American Church is in trouble. Second, because it offers not simply a diagnosis but a clear treatment and potent cure. There Re-formation is possible. It will not come cheaply, but it is available. And third, the messenger is living the message in front of us, and the validity of the messenger urges us to seriously ponder the urgency of his message.

I believe the years ahead of us will reveal Wayman Ming Jr. as one of Christ's chief shepherds and leaders of this generation, certainly in America, and with global impact. He is a trustworthy messenger who is living His message. This potent book is a serious remedy for our times. All that is necessary now is for those of us with "ears to hear" to draw deeply from its lessons, and together begin to re-vision Christ's covenantal call on our lives in this generation. I am committing myself to the call of re-formation. I pray that many will join us.

DR. ROBERT STEARNS
Eagles' Wings Ministries

A CALL FOR SPIRITUAL RE-FORMATION!

I pray you let us probe the consciences of our hearers; let us thunder forth the law and the Gospel of God until our voices reach the capital of this nation.... If immorality prevails in the land, the fault is ours in a great degree. If there is a decay of conscience, the pulpit is responsible for it. Let us not ignore this fact my dear brethren, but let us lay it to heart and be thoroughly awake to our responsibility in respect to the morals of this nation.

—CHARLES FINNEY[1]

What a clarion call for spiritual re-formation! During these last days, is it possible that the devil has tricked us into a role reversal? Is it possible that the Church is now on the defensive instead of the offensive? How often do we see sincere Christians walking around in a defeated daze with a defeated mentality saying, "The devil has been after me all week long"? If we are not careful, we play the role of the cowardly lion in *The Wizard of Oz*. We don't feel like we have the power or authority to roar.

The words *revival* and *renewal* are bantered about in sermonic poetry as commonplace expressions of spiritual dissatisfaction. And yet, are revival and renewal really enough? According to *Webster's*, *revival* is about "reviving what is dead." In my opinion, the Church is not dead. There are signs of life everywhere that Christ is seen as "lifted up."

Renewal involves "making something new again." One could certainly make the argument that the Church needs to experience a "washing of the water of the Word" to become fresh and renewed in Spirit. However, is renewal really enough? Renewal still involves experiencing what was previously experienced in days gone by. I would contend that the Church must have a spiritual *re-formation* to become what we have not yet experienced! A spiritual, moral, and social change that produces a new and improved version of the Church!

Do you remember when Moses was out minding his own business, keeping watch over his flock, and God showed up in a burning bush? What caused God to show up in the middle of the desert? What caused Him to interrupt Moses's life and put on a fireworks display for only one man? The need for re-formation! In Exodus, the Lord said:

> *I have surely seen the oppression of My people who are in Egypt, and have heard their cry because of their taskmasters, for I know their sorrows. So I have come down to deliver them out of the hand of the Egyptians...* (Exodus 3:7-8).

This book, *Re-Forming a New You*, involves exploring the potential of a new, improved spiritual life in practical Christian living and experiencing the coming of the Christ to deliver us out of the hand of spiritual bondage! If genuine spiritual re-formation occurs, it will be experienced in our hearts, at home, and in ministry.

Fortunately, the Bible declares that a mighty throng will one day stand in Heaven declaring that they *"overcame him by the blood of the Lamb and by the word of their testimony"* (Rev. 12:11). The blood of the Cross seals the devil's defeat, and the word of our testimony seals his retreat. This is good news! *There will be a spiritual re-formation!* Let's consider the possibilities today!

ENDNOTE

1. Finney, Charles. "The Seared Conscience." *The Oberlin Evangelist*, 1965.

RE›FORMING YOUR HEART!

CHAPTER 1

OVERCOMING YOUR FAILURES

>> Biblical Challenge—GET OUT OF THE CAVE

>> Biblical Example—ELIJAH

And there he went into a cave, and spent the night in that place; and behold, the word of the Lord came to him, and He said to him, "What are you doing here, Elijah?" (1 Kings 19:9)

In our present day, some Americans are certainly viewing our nation with a "dark cloud" attitude. The aftermath of economic recession and high unemployment has left Americans in a state of uncertainty. Mounting tension in the Middle East and possible terrorist attacks have left many shaking their heads. Discouragement and depression in the form of dark clouds seems to be hovering over many churches, and very few seem to understand why.

I certainly went through my own time of depression. Just like Elijah, I found myself in a deep, dark cave saying, *"Now, Lord, take*

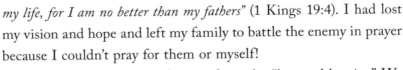

my life, for I am no better than my fathers" (1 Kings 19:4). I had lost my vision and hope and left my family to battle the enemy in prayer because I couldn't pray for them or myself!

Sooner or later, most of us confront the "betrayal barrier." We feel like we've been betrayed by God or that He isn't really interested in where we are. It is easy to hide out in a cave or end up with a despondent attitude, believing we are headed toward the cave, still in the cave, or coming out of the cave in a never-ending cycle.

My prayer is that you will have such a re-formation of heart that the cave will seem like a fading memory, and the failures of the past will no longer haunt you and taunt you with guilt and condemnation. Your failures tend to work that way. They try to keep you locked in the prison of your past so your present becomes myopic and your future becomes meaningless. As you will see, Elijah the prophet became a prime example of this.

Elijah lived during a time that desperately needed spiritual re-formation. A dark cloud hovered over the people of God. Wicked King Ahab and controlling Queen Jezebel were leading the nation of Israel down a sinister pathway of idolatry and false religion. Altars were being erected to the false god Baal. The prophets of God were being massacred by Jezebel. The Bible even declares that Ahab provoked the anger of the Lord and did more evil in the sight of the Lord than all the kings of Israel did who were before him.

Yet, God brought a spiritual re-former to the stage—a prophet who was not ashamed of his God. Elijah would stand with unabashed boldness and say:

> *How long will you falter between two opinions? If the Lord is God, follow Him; but if Baal, follow him* (1 Kings 18:21).

On the top of Mount Carmel, Elijah called fire down from the heavens, executed the prophets of Baal, and persevered in fervent prayer until God provided rain after three and a half years of drought.

What an amazing feat when Elijah outran Ahab's chariot to the gate of Jezreel and nodded at him as if to say, "I just want to remind you that God is still God, and the events on Mount Carmel are not a fading memory." Elijah was on the brink of ushering in a time of re-formation to his people. Just one stronghold remained—wicked Queen Jezebel. Surely, if God sent fire from Heaven and rain after three and a half years, He would handle one small, ungodly, arrogant woman. She was all that was left!

Yet at the very moment God was about to do His thing, Elijah fled from Jezebel, slept under a broom bush, and wound up in the cave. As we study the context of this unfortunate situation, Elijah reveals some specific signs that we should look for when we are heading toward the cave of depression.

SIGNS OF GOING TOWARD THE CAVE

First of all, Elijah *"arose and ran for his life"* (1 Kings 19:3). He allowed the personal threats of Jezebel to intimidate him and change his focus. He became more concerned about his own safety than the re-formation of his people. Focusing on yourself is the first sign that you are headed toward the cave.

1. You focus on yourself!

Self loves to vote for self. Self opposes everything God proposes. If you let yourself, self will set the agenda and your emotions will take supremacy over the purposes and plans of God. Why? Because self demands that you do everything yourself! Toddlers have that problem. They put their shirt and pants on backward because they want to do it themselves. No wonder Jesus said, *"Whoever desires to come after Me, let him deny himself, and take up his cross, and follow Me"* (Mark 8:34).

Christ asks for an incredible commitment. He asks for an absolute denial of self and an absolute obedience to Him. That is what it means to "take up your cross." I've heard people say that sickness is their cross or their boss is their cross. Those things are not their cross. The heaviest cross that you will ever carry is denying, ignoring, and disowning yourself and cleaving to Christ.

This is the greatest challenge to seeing re-formation of heart. You have to die to self to live a higher quality of life, and self is satisfied with the status quo, hating re-formation. Yet, if you commit to the principle of "He must increase and I must decrease," you overcome the first indication that you are headed toward the cave, which is focusing on yourself (see John 3:30).

2. You lose your praise!

Losing your praise is the second sign. You lose your attitude of gratitude and find it difficult to do what the psalmist declared when he said: *"I will praise the Lord with my whole heart"* (Ps. 111:1).

Re-forming your heart involves your whole heart. There are no restricted places of the heart that are untouchable. "No Trespassing" signs are not conveniently placed to keep God and others out of your life. I've been there and done that. I know what it's like to pastor a growing and influential church in the city, only to end up in the cave of depression, locking others out of my daily existence. When I had restricted areas in my heart, I moved from an attitude of gratitude to a place of barrenness and discouragement.

Elijah was in a similar place:

> *He...went to Beersheba, which belongs to Judah, and left his servant there. But he himself went a day's journey into the wilderness...* (1 Kings 19:3-4).

Did you catch what happened here? Elijah left Judah behind and went into the wilderness.

The meaning of *Judah* in the Hebrew text is "praise."[1] The tribe of Judah was known as the "praise" tribe, and whenever the children of Israel would journey, they were led by Judah. So when Elijah left his servant behind in Judah and went into the wilderness, he symbolically left his praise behind. You know that you are headed toward the cave when you lose your praise.

3. You check out spiritually!

It's dangerous to check out spiritually! When you check out spiritually, you place no value on life. Martin Luther King Jr. lost his grandmother, to whom he was very close, and he became so distraught that he threw himself out of a second-story window in an apparent suicide attempt.[2] Checking out spiritually can cause you to go over the edge.

Elijah found himself in that place:

> *And he prayed that he might die, and said, "It is enough! Now, Lord, take my life, for I am no better than my fathers!"* (1 Kings 19:4)

Did you notice why Elijah wanted to die? He had lost his dream of making a difference. He was saying, "If I can't do any better than my fathers or impact my generation in a greater way than my predecessors, I might as well give up."

Don't miss this sign of depression. When you begin losing your dream for making a difference, you begin checking out spiritually. You lose your motivation to act upon the plans and purposes of God.

Moses wandered around the wilderness for 40 years with a bunch of murmuring complainers, but he did it because he had a dream of the Promised Land. When God finally told him that he wouldn't see the Promised Land, he died. He checked out.

What will compel you to overcome the failures in your life? Your dream! You will be inspired to confront every stronghold that

stands in front of your dream. People who have a dream check in, and people who lose their dream check out. They end up saying, "I'm no better off than my fathers. This is status quo as usual."

The great thing about God is that even when you check out, He checks in. He will show up and sustain you just like the angel did for Elijah:

> *...Suddenly an angel touched him, and said to him, "Arise and eat." Then he looked, and there by his head was a cake baked on coals, and a jar of water. So he ate and drank, and lay down again* (1 Kings 19:5-6).

You may not be able to do anything else but arise and eat! Your failures may cause you to feel like you are unable to get out of bed or face another day. Yet that's when God loves to show up. He will reveal Himself in a "supernatural, surprise-me moment."

In fact, re-formation of the heart really begins with a "supernatural, surprise-me moment." God shows up in a burning bush to Moses or in a bright light to Paul, and re-formation of heart begins. And when God shows up, as in the situation with Elijah, He always provides the good stuff. He doesn't serve cold weenies and beans. He provides a cake baked on coals of fire and a jar of refreshing water. He serves up the good stuff to reaffirm how valuable you are in His sight.

God even served it to Elijah twice. That's what you call God's "Second Mile Principle"—loving you so much that He is willing to travel the second mile for you. He will go the second mile to save you, forgive you, heal you, and restore you. When you don't deserve it, He will still do it again. What an example of our God of the second mile!

Now watch what happens to Elijah at this moment in the situation. The angel says, *"Arise and eat, because the journey is too great for you"* (1 Kings 19:7). At this point the question is: "What journey is the angel referring to? The journey to Mount Horeb and the cave of depression or the journey back to Jezreel to take care of Jezebel?"

I believe the angel was referring to the journey back to Jezreel, because when Elijah goes to Mount Horeb, God asks him, *"What are you doing here?"* (1 Kings 19:9). The implication is that God was expecting him to go back to Jezreel rather than the cave. The last remaining piece of unfinished business for true revival for Elijah's people was back in Jezreel, yet Elijah chose the cave.

Even after Elijah ended up in the cave, God continued to give him a choice. He could get out of the cave and fulfill the plan of God or remain in the cave and hide from the plan of God. Spiritual re-formers are faced with the same challenge—to get out of the cave or stay in the cave. Elijah made the wrong choice. He decided to hide out in the cave.

4. You hide out in the cave!

> *He* [Elijah] *went into a cave, and spent the night in that place; and behold, the word of the Lord came to him, and He said to him, "What are you doing here Elijah?" So he said, "I have been very zealous for the Lord God of hosts; for the children of Israel have forsaken Your covenant, torn down Your altars, and killed Your prophets with a sword..."* (1 Kings 19:9-10).

Hiding in the cave will cause you to justify your actions: "God, I know You understand. I'm here at Mount Horeb, Your mountain, oh God. This is better than facing Jezebel anyway." How many Christians love justifying their inactivity by using their prayer closet as an excuse? Elijah was no different. He was not in his prayer closet to meet with God; he was there because he was hiding from Jezebel.

One may say, "How do you know when you are turning your prayer closet into a hideout?" Here is a telltale sign. You begin

pointing at everyone else: "They have forsaken Your covenant. They have torn down Your altars. They have killed Your prophets with a sword. They! They! They!"

An effective prayer closet has nothing to do with pointing to the faults of everyone else. One of the easiest places to become superficial and pseudo-spiritual is in your prayer closet. When you have filled your prayer closet with a bunch of "theys" and "thems," you have turned your prayer closet into a deep, dark cave! You no longer have a secret place but a hideout, and you end up moving into a state of self-pity.

5. You throw a pity party!

I've attended a few personal pity parties myself, and they're no fun at all. You end up feeling worse rather than better. The only person who ever attended my pity party was my wife, and she only attended because I dragged her along.

Elijah threw his own pity party: *"I alone am left; and they seek to take my life"* (1 Kings 19:10). When you're living through a personal pity party, you become isolated from everyone else, and the more you celebrate your self-pity, the deeper you go into depression

There was another man who threw great pity parties. His name was Jonah. God told Jonah to preach to the most evil city of his day—Nineveh. The people in Nineveh hated God and worshiped all kinds of idols, and Jonah had no desire to go there. So just like Elijah, he ran. He jumped on a boat and headed the opposite direction. Unfortunately, a whole lot of stuff went wrong, and Jonah found himself in Nineveh anyway.

To his frustration, the people of Nineveh listened to his message and changed their ways. They had been his enemy and the enemy of his people, but they experienced spiritual re-formation.

At the end of the story, we find Jonah sulking around and sitting under a plant outside the city. He's upset at God for delivering the people of Nineveh, and he's upset at this poor plant because it has shriveled up and died, ceasing to give him any shade. He throws himself a pity party, and right in the midst of it, God speaks:

> *You have had pity on the plant for which you have not labored, nor made it grow, which came up in a night and perished in a night. And should I not pity Nineveh, that great city, in which are more than one hundred and twenty thousand persons who cannot discern between their right hand and their left—and much livestock?* (Jonah 4:10-11)

Self-pity is the final sign that you have arrived at the cave because you can wind up having more pity for a plant than for 120,000 people who need God.

KEYS FOR GETTING OUT OF THE CAVE

The good news is that there is a way out of your pity party and the cave of depression. In the words of the familiar saying, "There is light at the end of the tunnel!" God is always faithful to re-form your heart if you give Him the opportunity. So how do you get out of the cave?

1. You repent and renounce depression!

When you are in the cave, you need to do more than repent for depression. You need to renounce it. To *repent* means that you turn from your sin, but to *renounce* means that you take authority over your sin. When I began to repent and renounce depression in my life, I began to say, "God, forgive me of depression. I renounce it in Jesus's name and ask You to restore Your spiritual authority in my life as a godly man, godly husband, godly father, and godly minister of the Gospel."

Overcoming depression is all about walking in spiritual authority and following the biblical mandate of not giving place to the

devil (see Eph. 4:27). When you give the devil place, you give him spiritual authority. That's what happened with Adam in the Garden of Eden. God gave Adam spiritual authority, but when Adam sinned, Adam handed his spiritual authority off to the devil. Notice the devil verifies this when he says to the Second Adam (Christ) later on:

> *All this authority I will give You, and their glory; for this has been delivered to me, and I give it to whomever I wish* (Luke 4:6).

The devil had obtained spiritual authority.

Before the first Adam gave place to the devil, the lions did not devour the other animals. Lambs had no reason to fear the wolves. Cobras did not have venomous bites (see Isa. 65:25). There were no diseases, poverty, earthquakes, or famines. The earth was not ravaged with murder, war, and death. However, all of this changed when spiritual authority was lost.

Whenever the devil can steal your spiritual authority, he will ravage your relationships, steal your health and wealth, send famine and pestilence and poverty your way, and strike you on the backside when you don't see him coming. The exciting news, however, is that there was a spiritual re-formation. The Second Adam (Christ) came along and restored what the first Adam lost, and he proclaimed, *"All authority has been given to Me in heaven and on earth"* (Matt. 28:18). Getting out of the cave must begin with repenting and renouncing depression, which allows you to regain your spiritual authority.

2. You praise your way out!

Consider the familiar story of Paul and Silas in the Philippian jail. The last thing that should have come out of their mouths was praise to God. If anyone was headed to the cave, it was these guys. Their hands and feet were tied, and their backs were bloodied from

a horrible beating. They certainly were in a position to throw a pity party for themselves (see Acts 16:25).

How many of us have experienced situations in life that didn't look too good? We felt like our hands and feet were all tied up. Our own strength wasn't sufficient to get us out of prison. The people we normally turn to for help couldn't help us. Our backs felt bloodied by the people who had beaten us and left us in pain. Many of us have been there, in a manner of speaking.

Yet we have a way out. Our hands and feet may be tied up and our backs may be bloodied, but our mouths haven't been gagged. We can still praise our way out. The enemy of our souls hasn't taken away our ability to praise God.

Now, like Elijah, we can choose to praise or lose our praise. Paul and Silas chose to praise God. They lifted up their voices so loud that all the prisoners heard them. They praised Him so loud that God sent an earthquake to set them free (see Acts 16:26). What a powerful revelation! Your freedom will come as a result of your ability to praise God in all circumstances.

God may sustain you when you don't praise Him. Just like Elijah, He may bake you a cake and give you a jar of water when you're hanging out under a broom bush! However, "being sustained" and "being free" are two different things!

God sustained Elijah, but He freed Paul and Silas! God fed Elijah, but He loosed Paul and Silas from their chains. In the midnight hour—in the darkness of my circumstances—you can tie me up, beat my back, put me in jail, and throw away the key! Just don't gag my mouth, and I will be free. As long as I have breath in my body and a voice to declare the greatness of God, I will praise my way out.

Right now, if you are thinking, *I can't deal with my drug addiction any longer; I'm tired of my struggle with alcohol; I'm finished with these patterns of sexual promiscuity; I want out of my prison cell of a job or my overwhelming debt load*, break out in singing and praise Him.

Walk right past the secretary into the office of the most powerful Being in the universe with your praise. You don't have to call for an appointment or wait for Him to fit you in. Enter into His doors with thanksgiving and into His office with praise.

King David lamented when he said:

> *...For I used to go with the multitude; I went with them to the house of God, with the voice of joy and praise, with a multitude that kept a pilgrim feast* (Psalm 42:4).

He recognized that there used to be a time when he attended the church house and made a joyful noise, but somewhere along the way, he lost his voice of praise.

Sometimes Christians don't realize how their lack of church attendance and gathering with the people of God negatively affects them. Just like David, their passion begins to wane and their praise begins to disappear. One may say, "How often should I go?" I believe that the more you rub shoulders with God's people who know how to praise Him, the better off you will be.

David went on to say in the very next verse:

> *Why are you cast down, O my soul? And why are you disquieted within me? Hope in God, for I shall yet praise Him for the help of His countenance* (Psalm 42:5).

In other words, he was saying, "Even though I am tired, disquieted, weary, and worn, I will yet praise Him! Even though I praised Him the last time I attended church, I will yet praise Him. Even though I praised Him at home every day this week, I will yet praise Him!" Your praise is an indication of hope, and when you place your hope in God, He shows up. In essence, you are positioning yourself on the mountain.

3. You position yourself on the mountain!

God said to Elijah, *"Go out, and stand on the mountain before the Lord"* (1 Kings 19:11). When you position yourself on the mountain, you position yourself to see God.

That's what happened to Moses out on the backside of the desert with the burning bush! When Moses turned aside and looked at the burning bush, he had a re-formation of heart encounter with God! It wasn't until God saw Moses leave His intended course or pattern of life that the Lord revealed Himself.

God's unchangeable New Testament promise says, "Draw near to Me, and I will draw near to you" (see James 4:8). To have a burning bush or mountaintop encounter with God involves drawing near to Him—changing your intended course of life to see Him and hear Him.

Have you ever watched people whom you know walk right by you because they were so absorbed in getting from one place to the next that they never looked up to see you were there? How many Christians never experience the greater depths of God because they are so absorbed with life that they never look up to see Him?

If God chose to interrupt our schedules with a burning bush experience, some of us wouldn't even know it. Our daily planners, Facebook agendas, and television time don't allow any room for mountaintop experiences. Sometimes God may choose to interrupt the schedules of our busy lives, but for the most part, He is waiting for us to look up and position ourselves on the mountain. He is waiting for the testimony of the Psalmist:

> *I will lift up my eyes to the hills—from whence comes my help? My help comes from the Lord, who made heaven and earth. He will not allow your foot to be moved; He who keeps you will not slumber* (Psalm 121:1-3).

We need God's help. We need God to show up. We need Him to whisper to our hearts in His still, small voice.

4. You listen to God's still, small voice!

God was trying to teach Elijah a lesson. It was a wonderful lesson—a lesson that He tries to teach each one of us. God was trying to teach Elijah that He desires a relationship established upon who He is and not what He can do. Isn't that the message God was sending in the wind, earthquake, and fire? God was showing Elijah that He wouldn't be found in the outer expressions of His power. He would be found in the inner whisper of His still, small voice.

Most of the time, we end up in a cave because our relationship with Christ becomes nothing more than a wind, an earthquake, or a fire. We're just tuned into God because of what He can do for us.

Whether we realize it or not, we live in a culture that emphasizes self-gratification: "What about my happiness? What about my rights? What about my dreams? What's in this job, this relationship, or this time commitment for me? What about me?"

Unfortunately, this selfishness becomes interwoven in our relationship with Christ. The simple truth is that too many of us end up following Christ because of what we receive from Him. He saves and heals us, and He helps us to be better parents. We are more successful in our business or ministry, and we are assured of Heaven and not hell.

However, real re-formation of heart comes when we love and follow Christ outside the grid of our personal needs. If we never make it outside of that rubric, what will we do if He chooses to stop meeting our needs for a season of time? Let's say that He allows you to go through the loss of a job or the loss of a loved one, and your life seems to be unraveling before your very eyes. If you're praising Him because of the manna from Heaven or the water from the rock and those things dry up, will you continue to praise Him?

Wasn't that really the core issue concerning the murmuring of the Israelites for 40 years? After all that God had done for them—releasing them from the bondage of Egypt, rolling back the

Red Sea, providing a cloud by day and fire by night, and so much more—they continued to point their fingers at God and complain.

How could they point their fingers at God like that? How could they complain and lose their faith continuously? Because they had become users and not lovers! They saw Him as a spiritual ATM to punch on until the object of their desire was handed to them. They were following God because of the wind, earthquake, and fire and not the still, small voice. That's why most of them never made it to the Promised Land. They didn't have enough spiritual revelation to *get out of the cave.* Getting out of the cave means that you position yourself on the mountain, and you build a relationship with Him for who He is and not what He can do.

RE-FORMATION CHALLENGE

God certainly revealed Himself to Elijah, but Elijah just didn't get it! Elijah never did finish the job. A man by the name of Jehu did:

> *Then he said, "Throw her* [Jezebel] *down." So they threw her down, and some of her blood spattered on the wall and on the horses; and he trampled her underfoot* (2 Kings 9:33).

Jehu had no mercy, no sympathy, and no compassion for Jezebel. While she was bleeding and dying on the street, he trampled her to death beneath the feet of his horse.

When you've got your past failures on the ropes, you deliver the knock-out blow. You overcome them once and for all. You don't let them up. You don't let their wounds heal. You finish the job, and you get out of the cave.

Past failures will try to get up off of the mat. The cave of depression loves to lure you back inside the power of its grip. You may live an overcoming life for an extended time, but then you

will have a rough day. Mr. Depression will show up at your front door, and if you entertain him or have coffee with him for even one moment, you will head back into the cave.

When Mr. Depression comes knocking, you must let him know: "Mr. Depression, you have tried to control my life for long enough. God has given me spiritual authority over you in Jesus's name, and I am not going back."

The good news for Elijah was that he finally obeyed the word of the Lord, and he was able to get out of the cave. To experience re-formation of heart, you won't overcome your failures in your own strength and power. You must listen to Him as He whispers in a still, small voice. You must listen to Him in the darkness of the cave.

I remember staying as a guest with a family one night and realizing that my room did not have a light switch conveniently located on the wall. I had to wade into the darkness to find a pull string from a light bulb. If you had been there, you would have seen me hit my shin on a piece of furniture and wave my arms around like a lunatic trying to find that pull string.

Once you have seen the light of Christ, you will do whatever it takes to turn on the light bulb. You will wave your hands in the air. You will repent and renounce depression. You will praise your way out of the darkness. You will position yourself on the mountain. You will listen for His still, small voice. You will do whatever it takes to *get out of the cave!*

RE-FORMATION PRAYER

Heavenly Father, I am ready to do whatever it takes to get out of the cave. I am tired of living in a prison of my past failures. I repent and renounce depression. Depression will no longer have a hold on me. I position myself to experience Your divine presence. I ask that You show up in a supernatural surprise-me moment and begin re-forming my heart. The thief has tried to steal, kill, and destroy, but You have come to give me life and life more abundantly. I praise You for being here right now and speaking to me in a still, small voice. I will bless You at all times, and Your praise shall continually be in my mouth. Thank You for getting me out of the cave, and thank You for re-forming my heart in Jesus's name, amen.

RE-FORMATION BUILDERS

Personal Evaluation

Elijah provides an example of someone who lost his way and found himself in a dark cave of depression. After running from his calling, he encountered the still, small voice of God. Allow the lessons learned through Elijah's life to help you avoid the cave or get out of the cave if you are already there.

1. At some point, most of us confront the betrayal barrier, which is thinking that we have been betrayed by God or that He isn't really interested in where we are. Are you currently experiencing the betrayal barrier, and if so, how are you handling it?

2. Are you willing to open up your whole heart to God and allow Him to begin the re-formation process? What areas of your heart would restrict you from doing so?

3. Past failures will seek to lock you up in a prison of the past. What specific failures are hounding you?

4. Are you seeing signs of discouragement or depression? If so, what are they?

5. What are the keys to overcoming discouragement and depression?

6. How can walking in spiritual authority help you live an overcoming life in Christ?

Group Discussion

Elijah provides an example of someone who lost his way and found himself in a dark cave of depression. After running from his calling, he encountered the still, small voice of God. Allow the lessons learned through Elijah's life to help you initiate group discussion concerning avoiding the cave or getting out of the cave.

1. After reading the lessons learned in the life of Elijah, are you willing to open up your whole heart to God and allow Him to begin the re-formation process? What areas of your heart would restrict you from doing so?

2. At some point, many Christians confront the betrayal barrier, which is thinking that they have been betrayed by God or that He isn't really interested in where they are. Give opportunity for personal testimony from those who have experienced the betrayal barrier.

3. Discuss the signs of depression.

    Focusing on yourself

    Losing your praise

    Checking out spiritually

    Hiding out in a cave

    Throwing a pity party

4. Discuss the keys of getting out of the cave.

    Repenting and renouncing depression

    Praising your way out

    Positioning yourself on the mountain

    Listening to God's still, small voice

5. Discuss the emphasis of self-gratification in culture and how it affects the atmosphere of the Church.

6. The children of Israel treated God as a spiritual ATM, punching on Him until they received the object of their desire. Discuss the importance of following God outside the grid of your own personal needs.

ENDNOTES

1. Herbert Lockyer, *Nelson Bible Dictionary*, (Nashville, TN: Thomas Nelson Publishers, 1986).

2. Henry Blackaby and Richard Blackaby, *Spiritual Leadership* (Nashville, TN: Broadman and Holman Publishers, 2001), 34.

CHAPTER 2

ORDERING YOUR LIFE

> Biblical Challenge—SEE THE FOREHEAD

> Biblical Example—DAVID

Then David put his hand in his bag and took out a stone; and he slung it and struck the Philistine in his forehead, so that the stone sank into his forehead, and he fell on his face to the earth (1 Samuel 17:49).

One of my favorite stories in the Old Testament is David and the giant—the destiny of a nation placed in the hands of a teenage boy. This story is a prime example of what can happen when a spiritual re-former is willing to stand and speak in the name of the Lord. Young David is a modern-day example of what happens when order and planning synergize with anointing and power.

While everyone else viewed the impossible, David viewed the possible. While everyone else focused on the way the battle couldn't be won, David focused on the way it could be won. While

everyone else looked at a ten-foot behemoth of a man with armor that weighed approximately 320 pounds, David was glued to the one place that would bring the victory. He could see the solution that could bring order to the chaos. While everyone else saw the giant, David saw the forehead.

Ordering your life is all about seeing the forehead—the one place that produces overcoming results. How many Christians live their lives in chaos because they can't see a way out of their issues or a way into an overcoming life? Rather than living with a focal point of victory, they live in a haze of defeat. They miss out on the revelation that God has an order for their lives.

David's experience with the giant allows us to catch a glimpse of how re-formation of heart even affects how we order every area of our lives. David was a man after God's own heart, and that affected not only his worship but also his stewardship of life.

ORDERING YOUR LIFE MUST BEGIN
IN PARTNERSHIP WITH GOD

Sometimes people can have the idea that they don't need God, acting like the woodpecker that was pecking on a tree. Just as it flew away, lightning hit the tree and split it right down the middle. The woodpecker heard the noise, turned back, and said, "Look what I did."[1] Without establishing a partnership with God, you will have a distorted picture of what you can truly accomplish. Your self-imposed limitations will keep you from experiencing God's "all things are possible" potential.

David certainly became the antithesis of this. Rather than relying on his own physical gifts, he depended upon God to propel him past his personal limitations. To the natural eye, there was no way that he could defeat the giant. King Saul even said to David:

You are not able to go against this Philistine to fight with him; for you are a youth, and he a man of war from his youth (1 Samuel 17:33).

King Saul recognized that David did not have the strength or the ability to defeat the giant on his own.

Actually, David had never even seen a battle before. He had simply showed up at the front line of the battle to provide his brothers with some Cheese Whiz and crackers and to celebrate his hero, King Saul. Yet while he was there, a giant of a man presented himself: *"…on hearing the Philistine's words, Saul and all the Israelites were dismayed* [Hebrew *chathath*: fell prostrate][2] *and terrified* [Hebrew *yare*: paralyzed]" (1 Sam. 17:11 NIV).

At times, ordering your life will involve overcoming some paralyzing words, such as, "You are nothing, will amount to nothing, and will accomplish nothing." Sometimes heroes, such as your parents, teachers, or leaders, will say to you, "You can't win this battle," and you will tempted to give up before you even try.

I'll never forget auditioning for a vocal music scholarship at the university I was planning to attend. The chairman of the music department heard my audition and tried to talk me out of selecting a vocal performance major. He said, "Now, I want to remind you that you will have to give a vocal performance recital during your senior year. You may want to consider an instrumental or even choral conducting major." Of course, he did not realize that his words were seeking to paralyze me from attempting to fulfill my dream.

However, I did not give up, and because I had entered into a partnership with God, I accomplished what he did not see as possible. Imagine the deep sense of gratification that I received when this same music professor came to me after my senior vocal recital and said, "I believe that this was the best male vocal recital that we have ever had at this school."

The reality is that your giant won't come and present his challenge just one time. Just like the giant that David faced, your giant will present himself every morning and evening until you deal with him. He will keep hammering away at you with his size and strength, day in and day out, declaring: *"I defy the armies of Israel"* (1 Sam. 17:10).

That word *defy (charaph)* in the Hebrew text means to "strip, defame, or expose."[3] Your giant will literally come to strip, defame, and expose you to a life of defeat and depression. He will come to strip you of your joy and peace—to relegate you to a life full of disorder. He will come to you and say:

> *Am I a dog that you come to me with sticks? …Come to me, and I will give your flesh to the birds of the air and the beasts of the field* (1 Samuel 17:43-44).

And yet, young David recognized his partnership with God. He knew that his sacred cooperation with God would enable him to conquer what he could not conquer by himself. No wonder he was able to say in a divine moment of spiritual re-formation:

> *You come to me with a sword, with a spear, and with a javelin. But I come to you in the name of the Lord of hosts, the God of the armies of Israel, whom you have defied* (1 Samuel 17:45).

David was confident in his partnership with God, and we must have the same confidence.

ORDERING YOUR LIFE IS DEPENDENT UPON A PLAN OF ACTION

Once you enter into a partnership with God, He will not leave you hanging without a plan. You will begin to "see the forehead." When David ran down the hill with a rag and rock in his hand, he told the giant, *"This day the Lord will deliver you into my hand, and I will strike you and take your head from you"* (1 Sam. 17:46).

When you read David's declaration, you can't help but wonder how he will take the giant's head, especially when he doesn't have a sword. Yet David already had a plan of action. He knew that he would knock the giant to the ground with a stone to the forehead, and he knew that he would cut off the giant's head with the giant's sword. Big tasks always come with detailed plans.

When God selected Noah to build an ark, He gave him specific instructions and orders. He said:

> *Make yourself an ark of gopherwood; make rooms in the ark, and cover it inside and outside with pitch. And this is how you shall make it: The length of the ark shall be three hundred cubits, its width fifty cubits, and its height thirty cubits. You shall make a window for the ark, and you shall finish it to a cubit from above; and set the door of the ark in its side. You shall make it with lower, second, and third decks* (Genesis 6:14-16).

During the days of Noah, a cubit was estimated to be about 18 inches long. So the measurement of the ark was to be approximately 450 feet long, 75 feet wide, and 45 feet high. If you will pay particular attention to the height, why would God specifically order the ark to be 45 feet high? Genesis 7:20 provides us with the answer when it says the flood waters *"prevailed fifteen cubits* [or twenty-two and a half feet] *upward"* above the mountaintops. How tall was the ark? Forty-five feet! How far above the mountains was the water? Twenty-two and a half feet! So, half of the ark could be under the water without hitting the mountaintops. What a great example of the detailed plans of God!

When God brought the Israelites out of Egypt, He sent them into the wilderness to give them order. He gave them special laws called commandments. He divided them into tribes and gave each

tribe a role and function with signs and symbols. He provided them with a cloud by day and a pillar of fire by night for order, and when they marched into the Promised Land, Joshua divided the land between the tribes so they would have order. God provided detailed plans.

In August of 1993, my wife and I were invited to come as possible pastoral candidates for a small church on the west side of Joplin, Missouri. At that time, our invitation was called a "try out," as if we were trying out for an athletic team or a music group. The 22 members of that small church were expecting us to preach our best sermons, sing our best songs, and tell our best jokes. Imagine their surprise when we passed out a five-page outline or plan of action.

We soon found out that we had frightened a few of them because we received 14 yes votes, 4 no votes, and 4 "I don't know (blank)" votes. Fortunately, we needed 13 votes, so we barely squeaked in as the new pastors. However, we began to implement the plan of action that God had given us, and within 12 months' time, that small church with 22 members had grown to approximately 200 in attendance on an average Sunday morning. We continued as pastors of that wonderful congregation for over 11 years.

Is it possible that we haven't really understood the value that God places on order and planning? Some Christians have certainly misrepresented the concept of being "instant in season and out of season" in all facets of Christian life. The apostle Paul said, *"Preach the word! Be ready in season and out of season. Convince, rebuke, exhort, with all longsuffering and teaching"* (2 Tim. 4:2).

The call to be "instant in season and out of season" was uttered in the context of communicating God's Word. All other interpretations become misrepresentations.

As committed Christians, we must be fluid and flexible to hold the new wine of the Spirit for every new season of time, but we cannot afford to live our lives as a disorganized mess, functioning with chaos and confusion. How many Christians would experience spiritual re-formation if they would simply "see the forehead" of their obstacles and have the courage to act upon what they see?

ORDERING YOUR LIFE WILL COMPEL YOU TO "SLING IT" AND NOT "WING IT"

Peter Drucker says that preparation "makes unskilled people without judgment capable of doing what it took near genius to do before."[4] Your preparation today determines your success tomorrow. Finishing what you start today makes it easier to finish what you start tomorrow. Killing lions and bears today helps you kill a giant tomorrow. Perhaps the ultimate example of how to "sling it and not wing it" may be seen in Creation. Every day that was created was created with order and purpose.

First Day: God Gave Revelation! (His Presence)

On the first day, God said, *"Let there be light"* (Gen. 1:3). God loves to turn the light on in those dark and lifeless areas of our lives—our relationships, family, career, ministry, and finances! He loves to say, "Let there be light." There is nothing like a "light encounter" or an encounter with His presence.

Second Day: God Gave Separation! (The Word)

On the second day, God separated the sky from the waters. He established boundaries so that the earth could function properly. Without form you will never have order! The reason why some people have a difficult time with order and organization is because they have no boundaries or lines of distinction! Fortunately, our heavenly Father sent the Word to provide those necessary boundaries for us.

What is interesting is that the second day is the only day God didn't see as good. He simply said, *"and it was so"* (Gen. 1:7). Is it possible that God knew the challenges we would face in separating ourselves from the daily grind of life to engage the Word of God?

Whether we perceive this as good or not good, it is a fact of life—it is so.

Third Day: God Gave Foundation! (The Cross)

On the third day, dry land appeared. God separated the land from the waters, which was necessary because humankind couldn't build anything on the water. In order to build, you need a foundation! Adam was not given a garden to organize in the sea; he was given a garden to organize on the land. The sea was too fluid—always moving and shifting. Man needed to be centered—to have something that was constant.

What is centered and constant in the life of the Christian? The Cross of Christ! The apostle Paul declared, *"But God forbid that I should boast except in the cross of our Lord Jesus Christ"* (Gal. 6:14).

Often in the Church, boasting seems to carry a negative connotation. Yet, God boasted twice concerning His Creation on the third day. The first time he boasted when He created the land, and the second time He boasted when He created the tree.

That's right! The tree, which is the grandfather of the Cross! The Cross was the solution that brought foundation for salvation, restoration for separation, and reconciliation for brokenness. The Cross was the answer for the second covenant and the Second Adam. When God created the Cross, He couldn't help but boast and say, "It is good" for a second time! Whereas the second day is the only day God didn't see the good, the third day is the only day He saw the good twice.

Fourth Day: God Gave Variation! (The Spirit)

On the fourth day, God divided the day from the night. He created seasons of change, and He created time with days and years. Aren't you glad that God ordered change or established variation as a constant in life? Without variation, life would be boring and mundane!

In the spiritual realm, God sent His Spirit to bring variation to our lives. The Spirit loves to keep us on our spiritual toes—sensitive to Christ and His will! The Spirit loves to blow in and blow out, producing a fresh breeze of faith. As John declared:

> *The wind blows where it wishes, and you hear the sound of it, but cannot tell where it comes from and where it goes. So is everyone who is born of the Spirit* (John 3:8).

Fifth Day: God Gave Proliferation! (The Name)

On the fifth day, God provided the proliferation of life! He birthed life—creatures in the sea and birds in the air. God is the progenitor of life and not death. The thief comes to steal, kill, and destroy, but God comes to give life (see John 10:10). The great thing about God is that He provided a powerful weapon to secure our future and hope—the name of Jesus. The name of Jesus allows the proliferation of spiritual life against the enemy of our souls.

Sixth Day: God Gave Domination! (The Blood)

Animals and humanity were not just created on the same day by coincidence, but they were created with an order. Humankind was given preeminence and was created to dominate over the animals and every living thing. In fact, animals became a source of atonement for humankind in the Old Testament. God declared that the blood of animals would be used to make atonement or pardon for sin (see Lev. 17:11).

But there was a problem! The blood of animals was only temporary. They could not do a permanent job. Humankind needed a perfect sacrifice that would do a perfect job. Jesus became that permanent sacrifice—the ultimate spiritual re-former. He re-formed the spiritual order and not just the physical order. He initiated the King-dom or King-domination through His blood.

Seventh Day: God Gave Restoration! (Our Worship)

On the seventh day, God gave rest and restoration. This was a big deal to God because not only did He rest on the seventh day of Creation, but He also made it one of the Ten Commandments: *"Remember the Sabbath day, to keep it holy"* (Exod. 20:8). God's day of rest is all about worshiping Him and thanking Him for His blessings!

Through the Creation event, our God was the ultimate example of what it means to "sling it and not wing it." The key to spiritual order is not allowing the universe of your life to function on the proverbial "wing and a prayer." As one of my college professors said, "If you don't want to fail your test tomorrow, pass your test today." It's amazing how killing a few lions and bears will compel you to take on a giant.

ORDERING YOUR LIFE WILL PRODUCE A POSITIVE REPORT

Isn't it interesting how King Saul changed his tune after David's victory over the giant? Saul enlisted him as the general of his armies, and he wouldn't let him return home. In fact, we hear that David *"was accepted in the sight of all the people and also in the sight of Saul's servants,"* and when the women came out of all the cities of Israel to celebrate, they danced and sang, *"Saul has slain his thousands, and David his ten thousands"* (1 Sam. 18:5,7). Everywhere David went, he had a positive report.

What kind of report do you have? Is your house ordered, or is it a mess? Can you show a guest your bedroom or would they have to step over clothes lying on the floor? What about your front yard? Some people have a yard that looks like that from the old sitcom *Sanford and Sons*. How is your yard representing the Lord to your neighbors?

I've heard people share the testimony that they spend hours a day in their prayer closet, or that they have the faith to move mountains. Yet, what kind of testimony are they really sharing if their lives are full of disorder? What kind of testimony are they really leaving their kids and grandkids?

Order is not just taught but caught. Are their kids catching their order or disorder? If their bedroom looks like a pig's sty, that's what their kids are catching. How can they teach their kids order and tell them to clean their bedroom when their own bedroom is unclean and filled with clutter?

If their car looks like a trash can, how can they expect God to bless them with a better car? If two-week-old, moldy pizza is still in the floorboard of their car, the roaches are driving their car. The song *La Cucaracha* (Roacha) is playing on their radio every time they get in! Perhaps I am overemphasizing my point.

However, re-formation of heart will produce order—ordering your house, car, desk, purse, and finances! When people say they don't like organization and order, what they are really saying is that they like disorganization and disorder. Most of the time, what they are really doing is seeking to hide the mess on the inside with the mess on the outside—trying to keep the focus on the external rather than the internal. However, the reality is that the mess on the outside is simply a statement of the disorder on the inside.

We have enough tombstones that have been erected with the epitaph, "Here lies the disordered and disorganized." We need a few more tombstones that declare, *"Saul has slain his thousands, and David his ten thousands"* (1 Sam. 18:7).

RE-FORMATION CHALLENGE

Everyday life is full of order. If you don't believe it, consider your morning routine. Most people have an order of the way they get dressed, eat breakfast, and primp in the mirror. In fact, getting gas involves order. Going grocery shopping involves order. Sending

and receiving mail involves order. Even receiving food at a restaurant involves a waiter or waitress taking your order.

Your life is a like a spiritual garden. It needs to be seeded, cultivated, watered, and weeded. All the vegetables need to be placed in particular rows and then harvested at the right time! Tragically, if you don't discipline yourself to order your garden, it becomes a mess. A reporter once asked the great evangelist D. L. Moody which people gave him the most trouble. He answered immediately, "I've had more trouble with D. L. Moody than any man alive."[5]

My prayer is that God will begin to whisper to you and say, "It's time to order your life." Perhaps God desires to re-form your relationships or your job or your house or your finances. But let Him continue the re-formation process in your heart.

Spiritual order won't come overnight. If it has taken a lifetime for disorder to come to various parts of your life, don't expect order to come quickly. God didn't order the world in one day; it took Him seven days.

However, just like David, walk down by a still, small stream and pick out five smooth stones! The solution won't be rough; the solution will be smooth! The solution won't be found in your purse, but it will be found in the Shepherd's bag! The solution won't be found in Saul's armor, but it will be found in your slingshot.

Because young David was able to "see the forehead," he was victorious. He became a spiritual re-former and brought deliverance to his world! As you order your life, you also will become a spiritual re-former and bring deliverance to your world.

RE-FORMATION PRAYER

Heavenly Father, I desperately need re-formation of heart. I need Your help to overcome the giants that stand against me and overwhelm me. Forgive me for trying to face them on my own and for allowing the paralyzing words of others to stop me from living an overcoming life. Right now, I need You and ask for Your help. Order my life. Bring re-formation to those areas that are filled with chaos and confusion. I want to "see the forehead" so I can "sling it and not wing it." Help me to have the courage to produce a positive report to those around me in Jesus's name, amen.

RE-FORMATION BUILDERS

Personal Evaluation

Studying the life of David shows us that re-formation is possible through a sacred partnership with God. When David confronted his giant, he brought order to a chaotic situation and experienced a great victory. Allow the lessons of his life to help you evaluate your own life.

1. Have you entered into a sacred partnership with God? If so, explain the difference that partnership has made in your life.

2. What are the current situations in your life that seem like giant obstacles?

3. Are you seeking God for a plan of action to overcome your giant obstacles? If so, describe what has been the result.

4. In what areas of your life are you "winging it," and what do you need to do to turn these areas into a positive testimony?

5. Prioritize the top three areas in your life that need to be ordered and provide a three-step process for each area.

Group Discussion

Studying the life of David shows us that re-formation is possible through a sacred partnership with God. When David confronted his giant, he brought order to a chaotic situation and experienced a great victory. Allow the lessons of his life to help launch your group discussion concerning ordering life.

1. Life is full of order. Discuss how this positively and negatively affects you.

2. Do you believe that people try to hide the mess on the inside with the disorder on the outside? If so, what are the indications that they are doing so?

3. Sometimes ordering your life will involve overcoming paralyzing words. Read the encounter between David and Goliath in First Samuel 17:41-50 and discuss the type of paralyzing words you have had to overcome in defeating your giants.

4. Through the creation event, God was the ultimate example of what it means to "sling it and not wing it." Discuss those areas of life in which you are more prone to "wing it."

5. Some Christians have certainly misrepresented the concept of being "instant in season and out of season" in all facets of Christian life. Read Second Timothy 4:2 and discuss the proper context of living "instant in season and out of season."

6. Discuss the statement: "Order is not just taught, but caught."

ENDNOTES

1. Anthony Evans, *Our God Is Awesome* (Chicago: Moody Press, 1994), 22.

2. James Strong, *Biblesoft's New Exhaustive Strong's Numbers and Concordance with Expanded Greek-Hebrew Dictionary* (Seattle, WA: Biblesoft, Inc., 1994, 2003, 2006).

3. *Ibid.*

4. Peter Drucker, *The Effective Executive in The Executive in Action* (New York: Harper Business, 1996), 565.

5. John C. Maxwell, *Developing the Leader Within You* (Nashville, TN: Thomas Nelson, 1993), 163.

CHAPTER 3

OWNING YOUR CALLING

> Biblical Challenge—WALK WORTHY OF YOUR CALLING

> Biblical Example—PAUL

I, therefore, the prisoner of the Lord, beseech you to walk worthy of your calling with which you were called (Ephesians 4:1).

Re-formation of heart becomes possible when we embrace the parameters of our calling. The apostle Paul stated as much when he wrote the above message to the Ephesians.

Paul was apprehended or captured by Christ on the road to Damascus, and from that moment on he became a prisoner of the Lord. His entire life changed. Those things that were predominant in his life—cultural background, family traditions, and religious orientation—all became secondary. He had reeled off his list of credentials to the Philippian Christians:

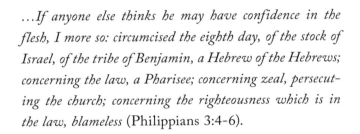

...If anyone else thinks he may have confidence in the flesh, I more so: circumcised the eighth day, of the stock of Israel, of the tribe of Benjamin, a Hebrew of the Hebrews; concerning the law, a Pharisee; concerning zeal, persecuting the church; concerning the righteousness which is in the law, blameless (Philippians 3:4-6).

Pardon the slang and exaggeration, but Paul basically said: "Ain't nobody got any better cultural, family, and religious cred than me. I came from good stock. My great granddaddy pioneered this country. As for my religious background? I was blameless, crossing every 'T' and dotting every 'I.' I've said more 'Hail Marys' and read more responsive readings than you can shake a stick at. I was a good Pharisee! As for my job? Now that's a funny story. I went from persecuting Christians to becoming persecuted myself. I went from being a thorn in the flesh to other preachers to becoming a preacher with a thorn in the flesh. All of those things that were primary became secondary to owning my calling!"

Unfortunately, some people still relate more to Paul's life before he connected with Christ. They haven't learned to "own their calling." They are still held captive by such things as their cultural background. Growing up Caucasian, African-American, Hispanic, or Asian has locked them in a prison of misguided attitudes and actions.

One day I was traveling from Tulsa, Oklahoma, and just happened to be on the same airplane as Bishop Carlton Pearson. Since the airplane wasn't full, we ended up sitting together. Although I certainly do not agree with his theology, especially concerning Christian universalism, he made an interesting statement to me concerning the African-American culture. He said, "We're living in the Promised Land of the twenty-first century, and some black folk still want to live in the wilderness...still want to live in the past."

What was his point? Sometimes your cultural background can become more important than your calling in Christ. Relating culturally can become more predominant than relating spiritually. And yet, didn't Christ break down the middle wall of partition between cultures? Cultural background should no longer take precedence over all else in Christian life.

The same could be said of family traditions. Some people become prisoners to their family tree: "This is the way our family does it, and this is the way we will always do it." Family traditions may be important to you, but not at the expense of your relationship with Christ. Jesus said:

> *If anyone comes to Me and does not hate his father and mother, wife and children, brothers and sisters, yes, and his own life also, he cannot be My disciple* (Luke 14:26).

When following Christ, sometimes you need to fall out of your family tree. Family traditions must not become primary and may even need to be abandoned at times.

Religious orientation can also become more of a priority than owning your calling. While I believe in the institutional Church and participate as a member within the framework of her structures and systems, I have also seen sincere Christians abstain from networking and connecting the dots of the Kingdom of God together. Sometimes religious traditions can keep you trapped in the four walls of the institutional church and take unwarranted precedence.

Of course, there are many areas that can distract us from owning our calling—position, prestige, power, and possessions. A young boy was on his way to church with two quarters that his mother gave him. She said that he could spend one quarter and put the other in the offering. He was running when he tripped and fell. One quarter rolled out of his hand and into the sewer. When he saw what had happened, he said, "Oops, God, there goes Your quarter."[1]

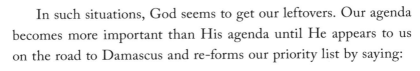

In such situations, God seems to get our leftovers. Our agenda becomes more important than His agenda until He appears to us on the road to Damascus and re-forms our priority list by saying:

> *I am Jesus, the one you are persecuting! Now get up and go into the city and await My further instructions* (Acts 9:5-6 TLB).

Am I suggesting that we destroy all of our cultural, family, and religious connections? Certainly not! What I am suggesting is that we, like Paul, become a prisoner of the Lord and of our calling. Walking worthy of our calling was so important that Paul literally said, "I beseech or beg you." Also, isn't it interesting that he wasn't talking here to the pastors or clergy who were serving in full-time Christian service? He was talking to the faithful and committed Christians of the Ephesian church who were in the businesses, hospitals, and public schools of their community.

WHAT IS YOUR CALLING?

Did you know that you have been called by God? Every Christian is in the midst of a discovery process concerning his or her God-given calling. Paul told the Corinthians:

> *But as God has distributed to each one, as the Lord has called each one, so let him walk. And so I ordain in all the churches* (1 Corinthians 7:17).

What was Paul ordaining in all the churches? That everyone has a calling! You may be selling cars, holding down a nursing station, teaching in a classroom, or flipping burgers, but you have been called by God. Also, your calling hasn't come from a spouse, a boss, or a pastor, but it has come from the Divine Being who created you. The exciting news concerning connecting with your calling is that once you walk it out, it will propel you

past living a Christian life that is only associated with attending church or going through the religious motions. However, first we should differentiate between our God-given abilities and our God-given calling!

When you were born, you received God-given abilities!

When you were created, God placed certain gifts and abilities in your physical DNA. God did that! *"God has given each of us the ability to do certain things well"* (Rom. 12:6 TLB).

Oftentimes, those abilities are simply shaped by your physique. Can you imagine a basketball player trying to become a horse jockey, or a horse jockey trying to compete in an Iron Man Triathlon? Basketball players were not created to ride horses, and horse jockeys were not created to compete in Iron Man Triathlons.

Some men have the form and physique that would allow them to pump iron and become body builders while others do not. Some ladies have the grace and finesse that allow them to become ballerinas while others could stand on their toes for the rest of their lives and never become ballerinas.

The point is that God designed every creature with certain abilities to excel in certain areas. A duck is meant to swim. A rabbit is meant to run. A squirrel is meant to climb, and an eagle is meant to fly. You are meant to be you and nobody else.

Consider the fact that there are approximately 6.8 billion people on this planet, and every one of them is uniquely different. Have you ever sat in a mall and watched the parade of people walk by? It is obvious that God loves creativity and variety.

Sociologists have shown that the average person has between 500 and 700 different kinds of abilities.[2] Some people are good at computers, while others are good with mechanical things. Some are good with numbers, while others are good with words. Some are good with music, ideas, or thought processes. Some have the ability

to cook, draw, speak, research, landscape, or build. Those abilities are not accidental but creational. They are God-given abilities.

Unfortunately, many of us are in touch with our abilities, but not with our calling; Paul didn't tell us to walk worthy of our abilities but to walk worthy of our calling. When we were born, we received God-given abilities, but when we were born again, we received a God-given calling.

When *you* were born again, *you* received a God-given calling.

If we're not careful, our God-given calling can be mistaken for our God-given abilities or even our occupational career. Here is the difference. Through our occupation, we connect our abilities to the world. Through our calling, we connect our abilities to the Kingdom of God. Our occupation allows us to do something of earthly significance, but our calling allows us to do something of eternal significance.

Some people may have the passion and ability to own and operate a business. They may have wonderful entrepreneurial skills and serve their communities with excellence, but their business prowess doesn't become a God-given calling until they connect it to God and His Kingdom.

Others may serve as doctors and nurses in health care facilities, caring for people who are suffering with physical illness. These people have tremendous gifts and abilities, but they remain only gifts and abilities until they connect them to God and His Kingdom and do something of eternal significance.

Another great example involves the excellent teachers in our public school systems. They teach children effectively and raise the level of education in our world. They contribute to make their communities a better place to live, but their excellence in the classroom doesn't become a God-given calling until they connect it to God and His Kingdom.

I'll never forget the public school teacher who approached me after church one Sunday. She shared her heartfelt feelings that she was too tired to teach any children at church on Sunday because she taught students in her elementary school classroom during the week. In as loving a way as possible, I shared with her, "So what you are telling me is that you are willing to use the gifts God gave you to make the world a better place, but you are not willing to use them to do something of eternal significance." She ended up reconsidering her position and walking worthy of her calling.

Owning your calling is all about connecting your gifts and abilities to the Kingdom of God and doing something of eternal significance. When you do this, a "blip" shows up on your spiritual EKG monitor! A breath of fresh air permeates your spirit, and re-formation continues to take place in your heart.

Peter, Andrew, James, and John enjoyed fishing for fish, but their lives were re-formed when they began fishing for men. You say, "But I don't know what my calling is." If you will begin connecting your gifts to His Kingdom, your calling will become clear.

The world is just waiting for some spiritual re-formers to own their callings and place the Cross back in the marketplace. When Jesus was crucified, He didn't carry His Cross through the back roads of town; He carried His Cross through the center of commerce. There's just something about "marketplace ministry" that ushers in spiritual re-formation to our neighborhoods and communities.

The real work of the Church doesn't take place by lifting up the Cross in the church house; the real work of the Church takes place by lifting up the Cross in the marketplace. We must exalt the Cross in the chambers of city hall, in the classrooms of educational institutions, in the rooms of hospital and health care facilities, and in the recording studios of multimedia centers throughout our culture!

Recently, I saw a man holding up a sign on the corner of a street in Branson, Missouri, that said, "You commit adultery when you marry the divorced." Pardon my lack of compassion, but such

comments won't draw people to a loving Christ. This world will not be changed by people holding up hellfire and brimstone signs on the corners of streets. The world will be changed when Christians own their callings and connect their gifts to the Kingdom in every level of society.

Isn't that what Paul did when he was captured by his calling? He simply plugged his gifts into the Kingdom. He went to places like Athens, a skeptical city filled with idolatry, and he used his education and oratory skill to take on the philosophers and intellectuals in his powerful sermon to the "unknown God." He used his boldness and assertiveness to preach before Christ-hating Jews, Tertullus the governor, Felix his successor, King Agrippa, and those of Caesar's household. Paul did not become a spiritual re-former because he was an extraordinary man; he became a spiritual re-former because he connected his gifts to the Kingdom.

WILL YOU WALK WORTHY OF YOUR CALLING?

What does it mean to walk worthy of your calling? It means that you will do what God said to do, and you will do it with integrity. There are four primary areas that you must overcome in order to walk worthy of your calling.

The first area is personal pain. When you are hurting, you will have a difficult time walking worthy of your calling. In professional baseball, sometimes players are placed on the disabled list because they are hurt and can't perform. They may be on the disabled list for fifteen days, or they may be out for the entire season. As Christians, we have to make sure that personal heartache or pain doesn't put us on the disabled list for an extended period of time, and if it does, we must do our best to get back in the game as soon as possible.

If anyone could have given up on their calling because of personal pain, it was Paul. He wrote:

I've worked much harder, been jailed more often, beaten up more times than I can count, and at death's door time after time. I've been flogged five times with the Jews' thirty-nine lashes, beaten by Roman rods three times, pummeled with rocks once. I've been shipwrecked three times, and immersed in the open sea for a night and a day. In hard traveling year in and year out, I've had to ford rivers, fend off robbers, struggle with friends, struggle with foes. I've been at risk in the city, at risk in the country, endangered by desert sun and sea storm, and betrayed by those I thought were my brothers. I've known drudgery and hard labor, many a long and lonely night without sleep, many a missed meal, blasted by the cold, naked to the weather. And that's not the half of it, when you throw in the daily pressures and anxieties of all the churches (2 Corinthians 11:23-28 MSG).

This is not even a complete list of his sufferings, because it was given before his imprisonment in Jerusalem and subsequent shipwreck in the Mediterranean on his way to Rome. Paul would also be imprisoned three more times; however, he did not allow his personal pain to keep him on the disabled list. He continued to walk worthy of his calling.

The second area that will try to distract you is displaced priorities. The demands of life can fill your schedule with the temporal rather than the eternal. Before you realize it, you can become so heavily involved in maintaining the family schedule, climbing the corporate ladder, or enjoying the latest fad that your calling ends up with the leftovers of your time.

The rich young ruler in Luke 18 certainly comes to mind here. He had accomplished many things. Just like Paul, he had grown up religious. He had kept all the commandments. He had grown up wealthy and had been successful. Yet, Christ shot through all

his accomplishments and directly addressed the displaced priority issue. Basically, Christ said, "If you want to follow Me, trade in your displaced priorities and come and follow Me." Just like many Americans in the 21st century, his priorities won out over his calling, and the rich young ruler walked away.

The third area is relational offense. Recently, I heard an interesting story about a woman who posted an advertisement in the newspaper. She was selling a brand-new Mercedes for $50. When a young man responded to the advertisement in disbelief, the woman shared the reason why. Her husband had left her for a younger woman and informed her that she could have everything except the Mercedes, which she could sell and give him whatever she sold it for. Her asking price? That's right—$50!

How often does relational offense distract us from walking worthy of our calling? Right or wrong, matters of the heart can become the primary issues of life and control our attitudes and actions. Paul experienced this with his young protégé, John Mark. Paul and Barnabas had taken young John Mark on their first missionary journey, but for some reason he returned home early after only making it as far as Perga (see Acts 13:13).

For that reason, Paul was determined that John Mark would not accompany them on the next journey, while Barnabas insisted that he go. The grievance became so pronounced that Paul and Barnabas went their separate ways. The Bible is full of godly instruction concerning relational offense that will help us through issues of the heart. We must not allow relational offense to put us on the sidelines of walking worthy of our calling.

The fourth area is low self-esteem. How many Christians end up doing very little for God because they struggle with a lack of self-esteem? They give up on doing anything for God because they don't feel worthy to attend the party. Unlike David, who continued to walk worthy of his calling when he was out tending his sheep, those who have low self-esteem become disenchanted because their brothers and sisters are partying with the prophet. They feel like everyone else is at Cinderella's ball, but they haven't been invited. Their brothers are lined up in their suits and ties before the prophet and their sisters are waiting for their dance with the prince, but they are picking burrs out of the sheep's wool.

Have you ever felt that way? If so, allow me to remind you that God hasn't forgotten you. While others may be looking at your outward appearance, God is looking at your heart. That is why reformation of heart is so important. Everyone else may be celebrating at the party, but God sees you over there crunching numbers, swinging a hammer, or giving the elderly baths because they can't do it for themselves. You may not see it yet, but God is already preparing for your arrival.

The prophet Samuel said to Jesse, *"Send and bring him* [David]. *For we will not sit down till he comes here"* (1 Sam. 16:11). Can you imagine it? Everyone is standing at attention when David arrives. David's brothers and sisters are dressed up and looking good, but here is unsightly David, still smelling like the sheep. When he walks in, he becomes the focus of the party, because there is just something about the called ones. Everyone is waiting for the called ones!

Here is the exciting news! When you become a follower of Jesus Christ, you become a card-carrying member of the called ones, and all things work together for your good. If you will not allow low self-esteem to win out and cause you to quit the race, you will end up with the "good life." You will stay on course and be able to say with Paul, *"I have fought the good fight, I have finished the race, I have kept the faith"* (2 Tim. 4:7).

THE FIVEFOLD MINISTRY GIFT TO THE CHURCH

However, we need to make a distinction between every Christian who has a God-given calling and some Christians who have

a fivefold ministry calling. Jesus stated it this way: *"For many are called, but few chosen"* (Matt. 20:16). The few who are chosen are called the fivefold ministry—apostles, prophets, evangelists, pastors, and teachers.

In a world where people tend to dismiss the fivefold ministry with disdain or skepticism, we must recognize the beautiful gift God has bestowed upon us. Paul declared, *"When He* [Christ] *ascended to the heights, He led a crowd of captives, and gave gifts to His people"* (Eph. 4:8 NLT).

What were the gifts that Christ gave to His people? Paul went on to explain:

> *And He* [Christ] *Himself gave some to be apostles, some prophets, some evangelists, and some pastors and teachers, for the equipping of the saints for the work of ministry, for the edifying of the body of Christ* (Ephesians 4:11-12).

Paul is extremely clear that the fivefold ministry gift was given to the Church *"for the equipping of the saints for the work of ministry, for the edifying of the body of Christ."*

The Cross literally became a crossroads for the world and the Church. When Christ died on the Cross, He gave the gift of salvation to the world, and He gave the fivefold ministry gift to the Church. The world received salvation, and the Church received apostles, prophets, evangelists, pastors, and teachers.

One may say, "I don't need a pastor." Why would God give the gift of a pastor if we don't need one? Why would God give the fivefold ministry gift to the Church to *"equip the saints for the work of the ministry"* if we don't need it? In truth, the fivefold ministry gift represents the work of Christ on the earth. When Christ walked the earth, He functioned in all five roles.

THE FIVEFOLD MINISTRY GIFT OF CHRIST

Christ served as the Apostle! The writer of Hebrews declared: *"Therefore, holy brethren, partakers of the heavenly calling, consider the Apostle and High Priest of our confession, Christ Jesus"* (Heb. 3:1).

The Greek word for *apostle* is *apostellos*, which means "to be sent forth." Jesus was the ultimate sent-forth Apostle. He was sent forth from Heaven to earth to represent the Father and declare, *"For I have come down from heaven, not to do My own will, but the will of Him who sent Me"* (John 6:38). Christ was the Apostle, and when He left He replaced Himself with the gift of the apostle.

Christ came as the Prophet! Peter said:

> For Moses truly said to the fathers, *"The Lord your God will raise up for you a Prophet like me from your brethren. Him you shall hear in all things, whatever He says to you. And it shall be that every soul who will not hear that Prophet shall be utterly destroyed from among the people. …To you first, God, having raised up His Servant Jesus, sent Him to bless you…"* (Acts 3:22-23,26).

Jesus was the ultimate Prophet who prophetically spoke that the Temple would be destroyed and rebuilt in three days, referring to His own death and resurrection. Christ was the Prophet, and when He ascended He replaced Himself with the gift of the prophet.

Christ was also recognized as the Evangelist! What was His primary purpose for coming? He said, *"The Son of Man has come to seek and to save that which was lost"* (Luke 19:10). Christ also declared, *"The Spirit of the Lord is upon Me, because He has anointed Me to preach the Gospel to the poor"* (Luke 4:18). The word *preach* in the Greek text is the word for "evangelize." The calling of the evangelist is to represent the evangelistic ministry of Christ. Christ was the Evangelist, and when He ascended, He replaced Himself with the gift of the evangelist.

Christ was revealed as the Pastor! When He walked the earth, He was unquestionably the Chief Shepherd or Pastor of His flock (see 1 Pet. 5:4). He also called Himself the Good Shepherd and expressed the heart of a shepherd when He saw the multitude as sheep without a shepherd (see John 10:11). Christ was the Pastor, and when He ascended, He replaced Himself with the gift of the pastor.

Finally, Christ was acknowledged as the Teacher! When Nicodemus approached Christ with some significant spiritual questions, Nicodemus addressed Him as *"a Teacher come from God"* (John 3:2). Many times, Christ was called Rabbi, which is the term for a respected teacher, and for three years He taught His 12 disciples. Christ was the Teacher, and when He ascended, He replaced Himself with the gift of the teacher.

Literally, just as Christ gave Himself to the world for salvation, He gave Himself to the Church in the form of the fivefold ministry gift! He functioned as Apostle, Prophet, Evangelist, Pastor, and Teacher. However, there was a significant change when He ascended to Heaven. Who would replace Him on earth? The Holy Spirit replaced Him from the Godhead, and the fivefold ministry replaced Him in the Church.

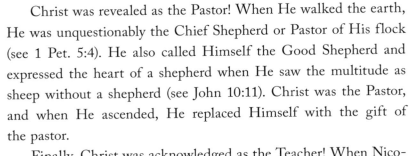

RE-FORMATION CHALLENGE

When God placed Adam in The Garden, He gave him a calling. Adam's calling was identified as tending The Garden and maintaining fellowship with God (see Gen. 2:15). Yet, Adam walked away from his calling and pursued his own agenda. He ate of the tree of the knowledge of good and evil. He messed up his garden, and God had to thrust him out of it. The only way The Garden could be restored was to send His Son to restore it. The first Adam turned The Garden into a wasteland, so the Second Adam (Christ) had to come and turn the wasteland back into a Garden.

Christ became the ultimate Gardener. He even said, *"I am the true vine, and My Father is the husbandman"* (John 15:1 KJV). Now we don't have to tend and keep the garden all by ourselves. We have the help of the Gardener. Christ said, *"As the branch cannot bear fruit of itself, unless it abides in the vine, neither can you, unless you abide in Me"* (John 15:4).

What is interesting is that when Christ was resurrected from the dead, Mary Magdalene was the first person to see Him. Who did she think she saw? *The Gardener!* (See John 20:15.) When you meet Christ, the first person you should see is the Gardener! Christ will apprehend you like Mary Magdalene and tell you to do something: *"Go to My brethren and say to them…"* (John 20:17). Or just like the apostle Paul, He will capture you on your road to Damascus and initiate your calling.

God has a garden or calling for each of us, and we must choose to walk worthy of our calling rather than following our own desires, needs, agendas, and plans. We may even have to overcome significant challenges. Perhaps the best illustration of this can be seen when Paul was stoned and left for dead on his first missionary journey:

> *Then Jews from Antioch and Iconium came there; and having persuaded the multitudes, they stoned Paul and dragged him out of the city, supposing him to be dead. However, when the disciples gathered around him, he rose up and went into the city…* (Acts 14:19-20).

Most of us would have fled for our lives, but not Paul. What would cause a man to rise up out of a rock pile of death and return to the rock throwers again? What would motivate him to move beyond the pain, the offense, and all the pity party issues? There is really only one possible answer. He owned a calling!

So the paramount question becomes: "What is your calling, and are you walking worthy of it?" If you are simply called to connect

your gifts and abilities to the Kingdom of God, are you walking worthy of it? If you are chosen to serve in the fivefold ministry to "equip the saints to do the work of the ministry," are you walking worthy of it? Allow me to lay down the gauntlet! It's time to "own your calling" and connect it to everyday life. If you do so, you are certainly continuing the journey of re-formation of heart.

As the apostle Paul later declared after listing his litany of credentials:

> *Yes, all the things I once thought were so important are gone from my life. Compared to the high privilege of knowing Christ Jesus as my Master, firsthand, everything I once thought I had going for me is insignificant— dog dung. I've dumped it all in the trash so that I could embrace Christ and be embraced by Him* (Philippians 3:8-9 MSG).

RE-FORMATION PRAYER

Heavenly Father, capture my heart with Your calling. There is no doubt that You have created me with gifts, and there is no doubt that You desire for me to connect them to Your Kingdom. I give all that I am and have to You. Whatever credentials I have obtained belong to You. Personal pain will not keep me out of the game. Displaced priorities will not redirect my time and energy. Relational offense will not disable me. Low self-esteem will not cause me to give up on the race. I will be what You want me to be, do what You want me to do, and go where You want me to go. I submit the garden of my life to You, the ultimate Gardener, and will walk worthy of my calling in Jesus's name, amen.

RE-FORMATION BUILDERS

Personal Evaluation

In the example of the apostle Paul, we find someone who was captured by his calling. Even Paul's litany of credentials did not keep him from forsaking all to walk worthy of it. Allow the lessons that Paul learned concerning his calling to help you evaluate your own calling and continue to the re-formation of heart process.

1. The apostle Paul stated, *"I, therefore, the prisoner of the Lord..."* (Eph. 4:1). What does this statement mean for you, and what are the implications?

2. List the gifts that are evident in your life.

3. Are these gifts connected to the Kingdom of God? If so, how?

4. Evaluate whether personal pain, displaced priorities, relational offense, or low self-esteem is keeping you from walking worthy of your calling.

5. Every Christian is called to the ministry, but some Christians are called to the fivefold ministry. How do you view your calling?

Group Discussion

In the example of the apostle Paul, we find someone who was captured by his calling. Even Paul's litany of credentials did not keep him from forsaking all to walk worthy of it. Allow the lessons that Paul learned concerning his calling to help launch your group discussion concerning evaluating your calling and continuing the re-formation of heart process.

1. The apostle Paul declared that he was a prisoner of the Lord (see Eph. 4:1). Discuss the implications of his statement for all Christians.

2. What is the difference between God-given gifts and a God-given calling?

3. Some people have a difficult time connecting their gifts to the Kingdom of God. What are the reasons for this?

4. Christ served as the ultimate fivefold ministry gift to the Church. What is the fivefold ministry gift to the Church today? (see Ephesians 4:11-12.) Discuss the purpose of this gift.

5. Matthew 20:16 states: *"For many are called, but few chosen."* Discuss the principle that all Christians are

called to ministry, but some Christians are called to the fivefold ministry.

6. Discuss how personal pain keeps you from walking worthy of your calling.

7. Discuss how displaced priorities keep you from walking worthy of your calling.

8. Discuss how relational offense keeps you from walking worthy of your calling.

9. Discuss how low self-esteem keeps you from walking worthy of your calling.

10. Are you walking worthy of your calling?

This would be a good time to pray over the ministry calling for each member of the group!

ENDNOTES

1. Anthony Evans, *Our God is Awesome* (Chicago: Moody Press, 1994), 315.

2. Rick Warren, *The Purpose-Driven Life* (Grand Rapids, MI: Zondervan, 2002), 242.

SECTION TWO

RE>FORMING YOUR HOME!

CHAPTER FOUR

BUILDING FAITH AT HOME

▶ Biblical Question—WHAT DOES YOUR HOME LOOK LIKE?

▶ Biblical Example—ABRAHAM AND SARAH

For I have known him, in order that he may command his children and his household after him, that they keep the way of the Lord, to do righteousness and justice, that the Lord may bring to Abraham what He has spoken to him (Genesis 18:19).

When you think of a house, you think of a physical structure—a building with doors and windows. But when you think of a home, you think of so much more. You think of family, privacy, warmth, and comfort. It is a place where you can wear your pajamas and feel good about it, or a place where you can go without makeup and not scare anyone. Home can be a wonderful place of retreat and rest.

Home must also be a place where Christ's Kingdom is established. The psalmist declared:

> *Your wife shall be like a fruitful vine in the very heart of your house, your children like olive plants all around the table* (Psalm 128:3).

Unfortunately, everywhere we turn, we are witnessing the tyranny of broken homes. Wives agonize over their husbands who never come home from work or who leave in the middle of the night, seeking love in all the wrong places. Husbands despair over their wives seeking the nearest party and becoming preoccupied with everything except God and family.

Parents weep because their children are under the devil's domain. Mothers tearfully visit their sons in prison. They know the pain of sitting on one side of a thick glass window, gazing at a calloused man who used to be a little tenderhearted boy running around in the kitchen. Fathers hang their heads in disbelief because their daughters are controlled by drugs and alcohol. They never dreamed that their daughters would hang with the wrong crowd and get hooked on physically degenerating substances. So now these young women are on the streets, selling their bodies to support their habit, and their fathers lie in bed at night crying buckets of tears because they're convinced that they've lost their daughters forever.

Recently, I heard about a missionary in Africa who returned to his hut late one afternoon only to be confronted by a gigantic python. He ran back to his truck and retrieved a .45-caliber pistol. Unfortunately, he had only one bullet in the chamber and no extra ammunition. Taking careful aim, the missionary sent that single shot into the head of the huge snake.

The snake was mortally wounded, but it did not die quickly. It began frantically thrashing and writhing on the floor. Retreating to the front yard, the missionary could hear furniture breaking and lamps crashing in his house. Finally, all was quiet.

When the man cautiously reentered his house, he found the snake dead, but the interior of the hut was destroyed. In its dying moments, the python had unleashed all of its mighty fury and wrath on everything in sight.

In much the same way, the deadliest serpent of all, satan himself, has already been mortally wounded by the death and resurrection of Jesus Christ. When Christ died on the Cross, He shot a fatal bullet into the head of satan, who knows that his days are numbered. In final desperation to thwart the will of God, he has unleashed all of his fury to destroy everything in sight, especially the homes of America. He hates the institution of the family, because it is symbolic of the relationship that Christ has with His Church.

I'll never forget a young father collapsing in my arms and shaking uncontrollably after he relayed the story of his wife leaving him and his children for another man. The devastation of the spiritual python in his home was disastrous.

More than ever before, we are in a spiritual battle for the homes of America, and waiting for someone else to take out the spiritual python is not an option. We must engage and do our part. We must build faith at home and catalyze spiritual re-formation.

God established this commission in the life of Abraham, calling him to leave a godly legacy in his family and transfer his personal faith to family faith. God said:

> For I have known him, in order that he may command his children and his household after him, that they keep the way of the Lord, to do righteousness and justice, that the Lord may bring to Abraham what He has spoke to him (Genesis 18:19).

Literally, God gave Abraham a picture of what his spiritual home should look like, beginning with "spiritual intimacy."

HOME IS A PLACE FOR "SPIRITUAL INTIMACY"

In the very first phrase, God said, *"For I have known him."* God had an intimate relationship with Abraham, which was extremely important for Abraham's family. In fact, Abraham had a practice of building altars. Just about everywhere he went, he would build an altar, modeling intimacy with God as a way of life. For Abraham's family, this was significant.

I've heard fathers say, "I never see my wife or children praying or reading their Bibles at home." The real question is, "Do your wife or children see you praying and reading your Bible?" Altar-building must become commonplace in your life. If prayer and Bible reading are a way of life for you, then they will eventually show up in your home.

Our homes literally become schoolrooms, and we become the teachers. Where do our children see a relationship with God modeled in everyday life? Where do they learn godly values, such as respect for their elders and sacrificial giving to others? Where do they experience the importance of having a solid work ethic and overcoming the lure of laziness? They learn these things at home.

One afternoon, my middle son Garrett invited a friend over to the house for lunch, and we decided to pick up some tacos at Taco Bell. While we were in the parking lot, there was a man holding up a sign that said, "Will work for food." When I stopped and gave the man some of our tacos, I overheard Garrett say to his friend, "My dad must have given him your tacos, because he would never give away mine." Although we laughed at the time, this was a great opportunity for a teaching moment to build faith in our home. I was able to share that the real issue was not whose tacos were given, but the real issue was sharing what we have with the less fortunate in Jesus's name.

Capitalizing on these moments is critical. Too many of our children have a shifting moral base, established by the media or our educational system. They end up deciphering what they're hearing and learning through the grid of our culture, coming up with their own value system. Oftentimes, God and biblical truth are relegated to the back seat. However, in our homes we have the privilege of countering the cultural grid. We can paint a different picture of God and biblical truth. We can change the portrait of God as an angry killjoy, absentee parent, or Sunday morning do-gooder.

Unfortunately, our family are not deceived by the kind of pictures we are painting. I certainly learned this lesson in an unforgettable way. One night I was sleeping, only to be awakened by my wife Kimberly who was having severe stomach cramps. She asked me to pray for her. So I rolled over and mumbled a few words of prayer and rolled back over to go back to sleep. After all, I had fulfilled my husbandly duty.

However, I will never forget what happened next. My normally sweet and supportive wife became righteously indignant, chastising me and saying, "How come you can pray with deep compassion and faith for everyone else, but you can't pray like that for me? How come you can believe God for miracles for other people at church, but you can't have the same faith at home?" She was absolutely correct. I wasn't building altars or modeling spiritual intimacy at home. Of course, shortly after, my commitment to building altars in the Ming home significantly changed.

Now consider what God said after, *"For I have known him."* He went on to say, *"...In order that he may command his children and his household after him..."* (Gen. 18:19). Abraham's commitment to spiritual intimacy turned into spiritual instruction for his children and household.

HOME IS A PLACE FOR "SPIRITUAL INSTRUCTION"

Some people say, "Actions speak louder than words." Obviously that doesn't mean that we shouldn't use words. There is something to be said about living it and teaching it. You live it out through

your actions and affirm it with your words. If you act but don't instruct, your home will lack affirmation. If you instruct but don't act, your home will lack confirmation.

Some parents relent by leaving all biblical instruction to the church. However, expecting the church to provide what is spiritually necessary for their children in a one- to three-hour time slot out of a 168-hour week is a false expectation. Although spiritual instruction at the church is important, it must not become a comprehensive replacement. Instruction from God's Word in the home creates a catalyst for learning in all other spheres of life—school, career, and church.

For years Kimberly has prayed with our kids before bed, and I have led a devotion time before school. This arrangement has seemed to work well because she enjoys spending some personal time with each of our children in the evening, and I enjoy a more structured family altar with all of them at the same time in the morning.

Because of this our children have learned a routine. At night they never go to bed without finding their mother, and in the mornings they come to the table for breakfast at 7:20 A.M., expecting to see dad sitting there with his Bible and coffee. What wonderful times we have experienced in the morning just talking about the character of God and His Word.

One morning, Garrett, who was 13 at the time, asked one of the most profound questions a young boy could ask. He said, "How could Jesus have been 100 percent man and 100 percent God at the same time?" For the next few minutes, we were able to talk through the fact that while Jesus was born, lived, and died as a man, He was perfect and without sin as God. That conversation would have never taken place if time had not been allotted for building faith at home.

On another occasion, I had been sharing some thoughts with our children concerning our five family values: 1) God first, family

second, and ministry third; 2) treat others the way you want to be treated; 3) always tell the truth; 4) do your best, and let God take care of the rest; and 5) live for an audience of One. At the end of our devotion, my four-year-old daughter, Gracie, came up with another value—"Throw a fit, get a spanking!" Her observation reiterated to me that even our little ones are listening and taking mental notes during times of our instruction.

Can you imagine the mental notes that Abraham's son, Isaac, was taking when he and his father walked up Mount Moriah to offer a sacrifice without a lamb? Isaac said to his father, *"'Look, the fire and the wood, but where is the lamb for a burnt offering?' And Abraham said, 'My son, God will provide for Himself the lamb for a burnt offering'"* (Gen. 22:7-8).

Yet, God hadn't provided a lamb when Abraham bound Isaac, laid him on the altar, and then took a knife to slay his son. This was a life or death moment of spiritual instruction, and Isaac was getting an eyeful. Would his father's promise that "God would provide a lamb" come true or not? Suddenly, there was a noise in the thicket. A ram had been provided.

How could Isaac have walked back down the mountain without the words of his father, *"My son, God will provide for Himself the lamb for a burnt offering,"* still ringing in his ears? Through spiritual instruction, Abraham had initiated spiritual re-formation for his son Isaac.

Often spiritual re-formation is a product of the atmosphere created in your home. If your rooms are always dark and dimly lit with spiritual truth, your children are easily overwhelmed with spiritual blindness. But if the lights are predominantly turned on and spiritual truth is readily available, your children witness the illumination of all that is possible in God. So, spiritual instruction must become as natural as flipping on a light switch.

When Kimberly and I designed our home, we designated where every light switch would be placed on the walls. However, when we moved in, we still had to get accustomed to where they were

located. We also had to learn what light switch turned on which light. At times I remember flipping as many as four light switches until I found the one I wanted. I'm sure that our next door neighbor enjoyed the light show. However, the longer we lived there, the more we became familiar with the lights.

The longer you build faith at home, the more your family will become familiar with the light switches. They will become familiar with the nature and character of God, the biblical values concerning marriage and family, and the importance of following Christ and His teachings.

Finally, after commissioning Abraham to instruct his children and household to keep the way of the Lord, God provided some specifics, *"To do righteousness and justice"* (Gen. 18:19).

HOME IS A PLACE FOR "SPIRITUAL INTEGRITY"

Our world is becoming an unfair and insensitive place. Doing righteousness and justice is becoming less and less of a priority. Our schools continue down a slippery slope of becoming war zones, and our churches are barely able to survive without becoming mausoleums.

Why do we continue to put our heads in the sand and pretend that our marriages and parent-child relationships are getting a passing grade when they may not be passing at all? Our families continue to be confronted with issues of spiritual and moral integrity while lacking spiritual and moral guidance.

Our society desperately needs an army of parents who will rise up and be a part of breaking the cycle of injustice in our world. How will we stop euthanasia from gaining a foothold in our culture? How will abortion or racial prejudice or crime or violence cease from overwhelming our culture?

As parents we must teach our children to stand up for what is right and just. When we are effective in teaching our children spiritual and moral integrity, we not only help them but benefit our society.

Just as Abraham, Nehemiah also realized the necessity of standing against injustice. The families of his city were threatened by a physical attack. So he made the statement: *"...Appoint guards from among the inhabitants of Jerusalem, one at his watch station and another in front of his own house"* (Neh. 7:3).

Nehemiah was living during a different day; however, with the events that happened on 9/11 in 2001, our own families continue to be confronted by the possibility of an imminent physical attack.

According to Nehemiah, guardians were not only appointed at the gates of the city, but at the doors of their own homes. In short, those guardians were responsible to protect against anything and everything that tried to gain entry to their families.

Is the message not clear for us? As parents, we have been appointed as guardians at the doors of our homes. We are responsible for anything and everything that tries to gain entrance—books, videos, music, Internet, etc. Our children should be protected from every Internet connection, television program, school friend, and childhood sweetheart who would seek to destroy spiritual integrity. This is not a charge to become the parental police but a challenge to lovingly make our homes a safe spiritual environment.

Parents may say, "I can't infringe on my child's privacy. He has his own room, schedule, and beliefs." Re-formation in your home will not come by managing a hotel where your children can come and go as they please. It will come by setting the parameters of what comes in and goes out of your home in a way that will build spiritual life.

You can respect privacy and expect diplomacy at the same time. If you have established a home that is founded on relational love rather than rules and regulations, there will be no problem establishing guidelines on the Internet or with television programming.

Your children will even partner with you in helping out around the house and attending church as a family.

Allow me to also encourage you single parents. God knows your struggle to serve as both a father and a mother to your children. You don't have to wait for a potential mate to come to your rescue. God will strengthen you as the appointed guardian over your home.

Building faith at home will cost you not only your time and energy but also your tears. As much as Kimberly was excited to move into our newly designed house, she still cried when she left the old house. The memories of bringing baby Garrett home from the hospital and watching the boys play baseball in the backyard made moving difficult on her emotions.

Memories turn a house into a home, and when you begin moving your family into a new spiritual home, you will encounter some tears. The old house is familiar and comfortable. But you can make some new memories—based on spiritual intimacy, spiritual instruction, and spiritual integrity!

RE-FORMATION CHALLENGE

When God commissioned Abraham to turn his house into a godly home, he had some obstacles to overcome. Do you know the story? Abraham and Sarah were "well-advanced in years," and God showed up and said that they would have a son. When Sarah heard it, she committed what I have designated as the two "L's"—she laughed and lied. But then the angel of the Lord declared, *"Is anything too hard for the Lord?"* (Gen. 18:14). In other words, this was no laughing matter because God can do whatever He chooses.

In much the same way, our homes are no laughing matter. How many families have given up on ever experiencing spiritual re-formation in their homes? On the outside they may not be laughing, but on the inside they are laughing at the dream that healing and restoration are even possible. Unfortunately, it's easy to toss the dream of a strong Christian family in the garbage and give up.

There have been times when I have counseled married couples, and I recognized in just a few short minutes that there was absolutely nothing that could be done for them. They had already made up their minds about leaving their marriage or giving up on their children. They had already made a decision to give up on spiritual re-formation, and the only reason they were visiting me was the hope that they might receive some kind of justification for the decision that had already been predetermined in their own minds.

Dr. Norman Vincent Peale relates his visit to a tattoo studio in Hong Kong in his book *Power of the Plus Factor*. During his visit, he saw several displayed samples in the window—anchors, flags, mermaids, etc. Yet, what stood out to him was the one, "Born to Lose." He entered the shop and asked, "Does anyone really have that terrible phrase, 'Born to Lose,' tattooed on their body?" The owner simply tapped his forehead and in broken English said, "Before tattoo on body, tattoo on mind."[1]

If our minds are tattooed with negative thinking, we become losers in our own minds. We see disappointment and negativity before we see encouragement and positivity. Our attitude becomes, "Don't look; you might see. Don't listen; you might hear. Don't think; you might learn. Don't make a decision; you might be wrong. Don't walk; you might stumble. Don't run; you might fall. Don't live; you might die." The epitaph on a negative person's headstone is simply, "I expected this."

If you lose hope for your home or you allow your mind to be tattooed with the idea, "born to lose," there is nothing God can do for you. The devil will stomp on the sandcastle of your home, and you will allow him to do it. Corrie ten Boom once said during

a television interview, "Are you dreaming? If you're not dreaming, nothing is going to come true."

Do you remember God's question to Sarah: *"Is anything too hard for the Lord?"* Sarah was laughing at the dream, but it was no laughing matter! She had given up on the dream of a family, but God hadn't given up. Looking at the dream through the eyes of impossibility did not change the fact that God was looking at it through eyes of possibility. If you will look through God's eyes, you will catch a glimpse of spiritual re-formation and see what your home is really meant to look like.

We need to have the spirit of the little boy in *Little League*. A man stopped to watch the game and asked the boy what the score was. "We're behind eighteen to nothing," was the answer.

"Well," said the man, "I must say that you don't look discouraged."

"Discouraged, why should I be discouraged? We haven't come to bat yet."[2]

The good news is that some of us haven't come up to bat yet when it comes to our families. The game may seem a bit lopsided, but we still have an opportunity to build faith at home.

In a special television interview concerning his faith, President George W. Bush once said, "Wherever I go in the world, I see the power of God in the family." May that be the testimony of what our homes look like—the power of God to the world.

RE-FORMATION PRAYER

Heavenly Father, I am in desperate need of spiritual re-formation at home. The spiritual python is unleashing all his fury to devastate my family, and I boldly declare that there is nothing that is impossible for You. Let spiritual intimacy increase significantly in all the members of my family. Help me to establish spiritual instruction that is consistent and effective in transferring my personal faith into family faith. May spiritual integrity be a way of life in my home! The obstacles that seem to loom so large must be destroyed to leave a lasting legacy. This is no laughing matter, and I submit myself to the spiritual re-formation process. Give me a dream for family re-formation in Jesus's name, amen.

RE-FORMATION BUILDERS

Personal Evaluation

God commissioned Abraham to turn his house into a home by leaving a spiritual legacy for his family and transferring his personal faith to family faith. Allow the lessons learned in Abraham's home to help you evaluate your own role at home.

1. Just like Abraham, do you see yourself leaving a spiritual legacy and transferring your personal faith to family faith? If so, in what ways?

2. "Spiritual intimacy" with God will build faith at home. What specific ways are you utilizing to build spiritual intimacy with God?

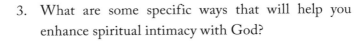

3. What are some specific ways that will help you enhance spiritual intimacy with God?

4. "Spiritual instruction" is critical in transferring personal faith into family faith. Are you really committed to directing your family in the way of the Lord? List some positive examples of this.

5. What spiritual instruction do you need to emphasize to bring balance in your home?

6. Nehemiah called his people to be guardians at the doors of their own homes. In short, those guardians were responsible to protect against anything and everything that tried to gain entry to their families. What are some specific areas by which you can take a more active role in protecting what comes in and out of your home?

7. What are some key attitudes and patterns of behavior that you need to set in order for your home?

GROUP DISCUSSION

God commissioned Abraham to turn his house into a home by leaving a spiritual legacy for his family and transferring his personal faith to family faith. Allow the lessons learned in Abraham's home to help you explore the role of parents at home.

1. If you act but don't instruct, your home will lack affirmation. If you instruct but don't act, your home will lack confirmation. Discuss the importance of balancing "actions" and "words" in Christian life.

2. Discuss the role of parents in breaking the cycle of injustice in the world.

3. What did President George W. Bush mean when he said, "Wherever I go in the world, I see the power of God in the family"?

4. As parents, we must teach our children to do what is right and just. Discuss those issues that need more focused dialogue at home (i.e., euthanasia, abortion, same sex marriage, etc.) that will help our children benefit society.

5. God may be orchestrating a much larger plan in your home. Discuss the signs and indicators that cause you to discern the bigger picture. This also may provide a good moment to initiate group prayer for discernment and wisdom.

Endnotes

1. Doug Dickerson, "Workplace Attitudes: A Lesson From a Chinese Tattoo Artist," CarolinaNewswire.com, February 23, 2009, http://carolinanewswire.com/news/News.cgi?database=columns.db&command=viewone&id=471 (accessed February 2, 2011).

2. John C. Maxwell, *The Difference Maker: Making Your Attitude Your Greatest Asset* (Nashville, TN: Thomas Nelson, 2006), 83.

CHAPTER FIVE

BURYING THE BITTERNESS

> Biblical Question—WHAT DO YOU DO WHEN
> YOU'VE MARRIED THE WRONG PERSON?

> Biblical Example—Hosea and Gomer

I will heal their backsliding, I will love them freely, for My anger has turned away from him (Hosea 14:4).

Broken family relationships are some of the most devastating relationships of all. They wound in ways that devastate us deep below the surface of our conscience. Unfaithful spouses, absentee fathers and mothers, and rebellious children cut right to the heart of our faith and test our commitment to Christ.

How do we deal with the brokenness? How do we overcome the pain and heartache of broken family relationships? How do we bury the bitterness in the love and compassion of Christ? These are questions that must be answered to experience spiritual re-formation at home.

Too many of us walk through life with a root of bitterness planted deep in the soil of our spirit because we have never answered the question: "What do you do when you've married the wrong person?"

THE PROPHET AND THE PROMISE

The prophet's name? Hosea! His profession? A prophet of the Lord to Israel! His story? Full of brokenness and regret! His story begins when the young prophet comes home from one of his many crusades. As he steps off the airplane after descending from the heights of Mt. Tabor, he is arrested by an awesome presence of God: "Hosea, I must speak to you concerning the infidelity of My people. I established a covenant with them and promised to be their God because they promised to be My people. Yet, now they have broken their marriage vows with Me and have had adulterous affairs with other gods."

No doubt Hosea anticipated that God was about to destroy His people so that not even a memory of them would remain. Yet, to Hosea's utter amazement, God decided to save them through the promise of His transforming love. What a merciful God!

Too many people today look at God through the jaded eyes of intolerance, as if God lives to discipline and correct them and that He has no tolerance for failures or mistakes. Yet, God proves time and time again that His love covers a multitude of sins and that He does not exist to smite them with judgment, but to embrace them with love. Hosea expected judgment from God, but God expressed His love.

The challenge for Hosea, however, was that God enlisted him to play a primary role in a real-life drama of His love for His people. God decided to give Hosea a glimpse of His divine love by providing a marriage companion. Now that doesn't sound so bad, does it? God gave Hosea the approval to get married, and He even selected the bride.

I will never forget when God gave me the approval to get married. He did so in two ways. First, He gave me an unwavering peace in my own heart, and second, an absolute peace in my parents' hearts. I was speaking for a church in Taft, California, and during the week I was there, the Lord woke me up in the middle of the night and proceeded to let me know (in His own wonderful way) that I would marry Kimberly Thomlison. As strange as that may sound, what was even stranger was that I had never dated her or desired to date her.

I can almost see the skepticism exuding from your countenance right about now, especially concerning hearing God's voice. We have certainly seen our share of Christians who use the words, "God told me," to appear spiritual or obtain personal and financial gain. Also, what do Christians really mean when they say, "God spoke to me"? Did God speak to them in an audible voice, or did He speak through other means?

I certainly can't speak on behalf of others, but God has never spoken to me in an audible voice. Although His voice has been so loud at times that it seemed audible, I have heard Him speak to my inner man. His voice has whispered to me in the stillness of my heart.

People who are not Christians have a difficult time understanding this concept. The apostle Paul even expressed this when he said:

> *But the natural man does not receive the things of the Spirit of God, for they are foolishness to him; nor can he know them, because they are spiritually discerned* (1 Corinthians 2:14).

This is why Christians misuse and abuse the voice of God by having loose lips with people who are not Christians.

Non-Christians don't understand the concept of "God spoke to me." However, we do know that God speaks to His people, as is witnessed by Christ's own words, *"My sheep hear My voice, and I know them, and they follow Me"* (John 10:27).

When God spoke to me concerning Kimberly, I heard His voice and I followed Him. After returning home, I shared my God encounter with my parents. Their counsel included a six-week period of prayer and fasting, because they knew I was returning to Joplin, Missouri, where I was an instructor for Messenger College.

As old-fashioned as it may sound, I had submitted myself to the covering of my parents and committed myself to a marriage companion only if they would give their blessing. This commitment was certainly tested at times because there were a few instances that I couldn't date someone seriously because there was no sign of blessing from my parents. In fact, I remember that on one occasion, I slammed the door on my dad and huffed and puffed down the hall because he was not complimentary of one particular young lady I was dating. At that moment, I was certainly not connecting Christ to our home.

In my situation, prayer and fasting were certainly necessary, because Kimberly lived in Hughson, California, and I lived 1,800 miles away in Joplin, Missouri. I could not see how it was possible to cultivate a relationship with someone who lived halfway across the country. However, I experienced the power of God's providence when I walked into the registration room at Messenger College six weeks later and saw Kimberly sitting at a registration table. Nine months later, we were married.

It is a good thing when God tells you to get married and then selects your bride. However, God's choice for Hosea was somewhat unusual. I can see Hosea explaining that at his last "Prophetic Crusade" a young daughter of Israel was passing out "Ten Commandment" tracts before church and singing on the praise team. But God had a different bride in mind. He had not chosen the choir girl from church. He had chosen Gomer, the daughter of Diblaim. He had chosen a prostitute!

THE PROPHET AND THE PROSTITUTE

Can you imagine the war that was being waged on the inside of Hosea? All humility disappeared and pride began to surface. Hosea was an orthodox Jew and a prophet of God. Marrying this woman would be an embarrassment to him, the church, and his people.

How can a prophet marry a prostitute? How can piety be attached to promiscuity and righteousness attached to wretchedness? How can the sacred connect with the secular? How can the divine hook up with the devilish? How can God get any glory out of a prophet marrying a prostitute?

Sometimes God doesn't give us a pre-flight itinerary to our final destination. He is simply interested in whether we will be obedient and board the airplane. He is interested in whether we will trust Him even when we can't trace Him. The reality is that a decision to obey God unlocks the door of His divine revelation. Just like Jonah, when we trust Him in the belly of a whale, we end up on dry ground. Just like Moses, when we trust Him before the Red Sea opens, we end up doing a victory dance on the other side of the Red Sea.

When Hosea decided to obey God, God unlocked the door of His revelation to Hosea. God showed Hosea that He would use him as an example of what it means to love the unlovely—to break His heart without breaking His love. God taught Hosea how to place value on the Gomers of life even when they are walking their own way and rejecting His divine love.

Now in the beginning, Gomer was flattered. She received a new wardrobe, and she changed her hairstyle. She changed the time that she would go to the city so she wouldn't be associated with her old way of life. Her attitude and outlook were brand-new.

After all, now she was a prophet's wife, and yet there was still a big problem. Gomer had left the old way of life because she made a commitment to her husband, but not to God. Gomer was caught in a carnal battle. Daily she was wooed by her old way of life, and daily she battled the sins of her past.

Is that not a major challenge for some Christians today? They make a commitment to a tradition, program, religion, and dogma, but they don't make a commitment to God. Consequently, when they have trouble, their commitment to man is not strong enough to sustain them. They must have a greater power outside of themselves to keep them and a greater authority outside of themselves to secure them. They need the power and person of God Himself.

The other problem that Gomer faced was self-righteousness in the Church. The Kingdom monitors showed up and began raising their voices immediately: "You are a prostitute, but now you can't do that anymore. Real Christians do not condone unbiblical living." The Kingdom monitors always seem to know the Scripture like the back of their hands instead of knowing it in the front of their hearts. Jesus encountered this continually from the religious elite who became furious because of His irresponsible habit of throwing open the doors of His love to the "whosoevers of the world."

In his book, *Letters to My Children*, Daniel Taylor describes an experience in sixth grade. At that time, boys and girls were paired together for certain exercises in class. Thank God this doesn't happen much today, but the boys would line up and choose the girls. One girl, Mary, was always chosen last because one of her arms was drawn up and she had a crippled leg. One day, the assistant teacher pulled young Daniel aside, who had received his turn to select first, and she encouraged him to choose Mary, sharing that Jesus would have done the same. Daniel relates what happened:

The faces of the girls were turned toward me, some smiling. I looked at Mary and saw that she was only half-turned to the back of the room. (She knew no one would pick her first) …Mr. Jenkins said, "Okay, Dan—choose your partner!"

I remember feeling very far away. I heard my voice say, "I choose Mary." Never has reluctant virtue been so rewarded. I still see her face undimmed in my memory. She lifted her head, and on her face, reddened with pleasure and surprise and embarrassment all at once, was the most genuine look of delight and even pride that I have ever seen, before or since. It was so pure that I had to look away because I knew I didn't deserve it.

Mary came and took my arm, as we had been instructed, and she walked beside me, bad leg and all, just like a princess…[1]

In the Church, we have a propensity to forget that God loves to choose the Marys of life. While Mary doesn't always measure up to our standards physically or spiritually, she is still just like a princess to God. Perhaps we should consider changing the title of our sermon from "Sinners in the Hands of an Angry God" to "Sinners in the Hands of a Loving God."

For Gomer, the spiritual sabotage of the religious was too much, and little by little she retreated to her old way of life until she finally left Hosea. Of course, Hosea must have had an "I-told-you-so moment" with God. When he went back to Mount Tabor, he must have said, "God, I told you what she would do. I told you that a prophet shouldn't marry a prostitute. I told you that I should have married that girl at the prophetic crusade. Now look at me, God; I'm raising three children by myself that You named Jezreel (punishment), Lo-Ruhamah (unloved), and LoAmmi (abandoned).

God, I told you so." Hosea was confronted with the question, "What do you do when you've married the wrong person?"

However, the unshakeable fact remained that even though Hosea had been criticized and had become the laughingstock of his people, he still loved her. Despite the rejection, abandonment, heartache, and pain, Hosea caught a glimpse of the heartbeat of God and how He loved His people.

Hosea gives us a vibrant picture concerning the way we must look at our own family relationships. At times we will feel rejected and abandoned, but we still must love and forgive.

Only when we come in contact with the unlovely can we know the depth of God's love. Not until we walk hand in hand and side by side with those who do not see as we see and think as we think and feel as we feel do we really learn to love. When we are confronted with placing someone else before ourselves, we are confronted with the depth of God's divine love. Not until we have been wronged by someone, and our memory is too good as we relive that offense day after day, can we really learn to love as God loves.

Hosea lived his rejection every day! Every day he raised his three children without their mother. Every day he woke them up and got them off to school. Every day he took them to their soccer games and band practices by himself. Every day he tried to make up the love they were missing in a single-parent home. Every day he worked two and three jobs just to provide what was necessary for them to survive.

One day, two monks were walking through the countryside on their way to another village. As they walked, they spied an old woman sitting at the edge of a river. She was upset because there was no bridge, and she could not get across on her own. The two monks kindly offered, "We'll carry you across if you'd like." The woman was grateful and accepted their offer. So the two men joined hands, lifted her between them and carried her across the river. When they made it to the other side, the woman went on her way.

After the monks had walked about a mile, one of them began to complain: "Look at my clothes. They are filthy from carrying that woman across the river. And my back still hurts from lifting her. I can already feel it getting stiff." A few more miles up the road, the monk was still complaining, "My back is still hurting because we carried that silly woman across the river. I can't go another mile."

The other monk who hadn't said a word finally looked at his complaining comrade and said, "Have you wondered why I'm not complaining? Your back hurts because you're still carrying the woman. But I set her down at the river."[2]

How many people are still carrying the pain of their past with them because they haven't set it down and let it go? If anyone could have allowed the root of bitterness to be planted deep in his spirit, that person was Hosea. If anyone could have lived the rest of his life with unprocessed pain, Hosea was the one.

THE PROPHET AND THE PURCHASE!

Scores of adults are living with unprocessed pain and suffering, and rather than experience spiritual re-formation, they continue to birth another generation into their own brokenness. Brokenness continues to be passed down from one generation to the next.

Have you ever considered what kind of fathers and mothers generally harm their children? The fathers and mothers who were hurt deeply as children themselves! The ramifications are significant, because if we have broken marriages, we have broken families. If we have broken families, we have broken churches. If we have broken churches, we have broken cities. If we have broken cities, we have broken communities. If we have broken communities, we have broken nations.

Perhaps our plight can be compared to the field worker in Queensland, Australia, harvesting sugar cane. He was cutting cane with a razor-sharp machete. The heat was oppressive. The air was full of flies, and salty sweat was stinging his eyes. As he bent into his next stroke, he suddenly experienced an accident. His razor-sharp blade glanced off a stalk and slashed a gaping wound in his left arm. Smelling blood, the flies began to swarm the wound because it was their nature to do so. Rather than going to the hospital to receive stitching and bandages for the wound, he wrapped his arm and continued cutting the cane.

Unfortunately, too many of our homes have become just like the sugar cane field worker. Rather than experiencing healing in our homes, we continue to bleed from gaping wounds and fight the flies. We would rather be wounded and hurting than healed and well.

We must not minimize the reality that family health is at the core of world health. What would happen if some parents decided to go to the hospital? What would happen if some moms and dads decided to stop fighting the flies and get some help? What would happen if some mommies and daddies decided to take a "time out" to be healed? Re-formation at home would happen.

Despite Harry Truman's role as president of the United States, he never forgot what was most important to him. When Bess Truman was asked what she considered the most memorable aspect of her life she replied, "Harry and I have been sweethearts and married for more than forty years—and no matter where I was, when I put out my hand, Harry's was there to grasp it."[3] During some of the most critical moments of history, even the president of the United States did not forget what was most important in his life.

One day Hosea was out in the sugarcane field (actually cornfield) and word came to him, "Gomer, your wife, is back in town. She is at the slave block, and they are selling her. She is wrinkled from sin and a shell of a woman. She is stripped naked and is shamefully sitting on the auction block, being mocked. Now is your chance, Hosea. You can get in the last word. You can say, 'I told you so.'"

Hosea grabbed his prophet robe and headed to town. The crowd was certainly waiting for Hosea to pay her back for all the pain that she had caused him—to laugh at her and tell her that she was getting what she deserved. The crowd was waiting for Hosea to get in the last word.

When Hosea got there, the bidding on her had started. "Five hundred to the man in the ball cap," said the auctioneer. "Six hundred to the man in the red tie; seven hundred to the man with the three-piece suit," he continued. Just as the auctioneer said, "Going once, going twice," a prophetic voice was heard from the midst of the crowd, "I'll give everything I've got for her."

The crowd became deathly silent as the auctioneer pounded the gavel and said, "Going once, going twice, sold to the prophet Hosea." Everyone watched in astonishment as Hosea purchased his wife, lovingly clothed her, and took her home. He had buried his bitterness in the depth of God's divine love.

RE-FORMATION CHALLENGE

So, what do you do when you think you've married the wrong person? What do you do when you've been rejected and abandoned? What do you do when you've experienced the heartache and the pain of broken relationships? You love and forgive and restore all over again.

There's someone who needs you at the auction block—a Gomer who is looking for your love, forgiveness, and fellowship. There are family members at the auction block who have value, even when everyone else has given up on them.

Consider the greatest love story ever witnessed—the one that started in the Garden of Eden. Humankind rejected God, and we were placed on the slave block, broken by our sin and separation from God. Satan was bidding on our destiny and eternity. As the Grand Auctioneer began the final countdown—going once, going twice—there came a prophetic Voice from the midst of the crowd, "I'll give everything I've got for them." In the words of the apostle Paul:

> *But God put His love on the line for us by offering His Son in sacrificial death while we were of no use whatever to Him* (Romans 5:8 MSG).

The greatest love story ever told involved Christ giving His life on a cruel Cross so that humankind could once again be purchased or redeemed, clothed with salvation, and returned home. Christ buried the bitterness in a tomb of resurrection power. Ultimately, Christ showed us what to do when you've married the wrong person. Let us become bold enough to follow in His footsteps!

RE-FORMATION PRAYER

Heavenly Father, thank You for putting Your love on the line for me when I was unlovely. You know the heartache that I have experienced in broken relationships, and I refuse to remain in the grip of any kind of unprocessed pain. Just as You did for Hosea, enable me to love and show compassion. Help me to forgive those who have hurt me, and if there are any seeds of bitterness that have been planted in the soil of my spirit, root them out right now. Let Your divine love wash me clean. I choose to buy back the Gomers in my life and experience spiritual re-formation in Jesus's name. Amen.

RE-FORMATION BUILDERS

Personal Evaluation

God demonstrated the depth of His divine love through the marriage of Hosea and Gomer. Hosea revealed the power of forgiveness and reconciliation in the way he related to his wife. Allow the lessons learned in this re-formed relationship to help you evaluate the relationships in your own life and family.

1. Who are the individuals who have played the role of Gomer in your life?

2. As you consider those who have hurt you in relationships, are you aware of any unprocessed pain? If so, what steps should you take to process it?

3. How have the Gomers in your life caused you to treat others, especially your own family members?

4. What steps do you need to take to be a catalyst of healing for your family members who ended up experiencing the collateral damage of your broken relationships?

5. What are some specific ways in which you should engage in prayer, Bible study, and relational account-ability to help you overcome any lasting emotion-al residue?

Group Discussion

God demonstrated the depth of His divine love through the marriage of Hosea and Gomer. Hosea revealed the power of for-giveness and reconciliation in the way he related to his wife. Allow the lessons learned in this re-formed relationship to help you discuss the relationships in your own life and family.

1. Unforgiveness toward others can easily establish a home in your heart. Discuss the signs that indicate unforgiveness is knocking at the door, seeking to gain entrance.

2. Discuss the differences between unforgiveness and bitterness. Then discuss the indicators that show up when unforgiveness has turned into bitterness.

3. Discuss the ways people can protect their heart from such spiritual bondage.

4. Once someone is free from unforgiveness and bitter-ness, discuss the ways to maintain freedom.

5. Oftentimes, God brings His people through recon-ciliation and restoration to help others through the same process. Is there someone that you might help

through the process of reconciliation and restoration, and if so, how?

ENDNOTES

1. Dan Taylor, *Letters to My Children* (Downers Grove, IL: InterVarsity Press, 1989), 13-17.

2. Anthony Evans, *Guiding Your Family in a Misguided World* (Colorado Springs, CO: Focus on the Family Publishing, 1991), 35.

3. David McCullough, *Truman* (New York: Touchstone, 1992), 564.

CHAPTER SIX

BLESSING YOUR CHILDREN

❯ Biblical Question—WHAT DO WE TELL OUR KIDS?

❯ Biblical Example—HAGAR AND ISHMAEL

Arise, lift up the lad and hold him with your hand, for I will make him a great nation (Genesis 21:18).

Perhaps you have heard of the old superstition from the East that encouraged parents to predict their child's future by placing a Bible, bottle of wine, and some money on a table within their child's reach. If the little one picked up the Bible, folk wisdom suggested that he would follow a spiritual vocation, such as the priesthood. If the child picked up the bottle of wine, hedonism would control his life. If the child selected the money, business and an entrepreneurial spirit would be in the future.

So as the story goes, a new father decided to give the superstition a try. He carefully positioned the items on the coffee table and loosed his little man to make a selection. The father was

confounded when his child put the Bible under one arm, snatched the money and the bottle of wine with both hands, and ran off. When the father overcame his surprise, he made the observation, "This is bad news. He's going to become a politician."[1]

We are certainly living in a unique era of American history. Our children continue to be confronted with the serious choices of life at an even younger age. Because of television and social networking, very few subjects are now off-limits.

Do you remember when Kobe Bryant of the famed Los Angeles Lakers went through a court case concerning accusations of rape and physical assault? You couldn't turn on the television without hearing updates from syndicated sporting news stations concerning Kobe's pending court case. Even preschoolers and kindergarteners were asking questions concerning Kobe: "How come he was arrested?" Or "Why is he in trouble?" Or perhaps the most difficult question, "What did he do?"

One day, my boys and I were catching up on the sports highlights when Kobe's case came up, and I will never forget when my innocent-minded sons asked the question, "What did Kobe do?" Candidly, they hadn't experienced "the talk" yet. You know—the one with the birds and the bees! But at that moment I was confronted with the question, "What do I tell my kids?" What I really wanted to say was, "We'll talk about it later."

Unfortunately, this is how some parents respond when challenged with difficult questions by their children: "We'll talk about it later," or "Why don't you talk to your dad when he gets home?" These sincere parents are sending a polite message to their children that the line of communication is closed, especially with certain issues. One of the greatest blessings that you can provide for your children involves creating an environment of open communication where they can talk to you about anything at anytime.

This time of open communication is critical, especially since conversations with sexual overtones have overwhelmed our culture.

One day I overheard a conversation concerning the music group The Bloodhound Gang. One young man referred to the lyrics of one of their songs: "You and me baby ain't nothin' but mammals, so let's do it like they do on the Discovery Channel."[2]

If you haven't noticed lately, people act much differently than animals. We do not snort and stomp around like bulls that have serviced cows in the broad daylight of the pasture. We have a moral fiber that advocates privacy and intimacy. Our children must know the difference and learn the sacredness of sexual intimacy in the marriage bed.

Kobe's situation afforded me an opportunity to open up the lines of communication with my boys concerning sexuality. I was able to share that a judge was holding a trial to see whether Kobe was guilty or innocent of having a relationship with a girl other than his wife. I was able to reinforce God's expectations for marriage.

The example of Hagar and Ishmael presents us with a portrait of how valuable our children really are. Hagar, the Egyptian maidservant of Sarah, had been thrust upon Abraham to conceive a son because Sarah was barren. The thought process of pushing your servant girl into the arms of your husband is certainly beyond my sphere of understanding. Yet, when the deed was done and Hagar conceived, Sarah regretted her actions, and Hagar and her son Ishmael became a liability.

Eventually, through the direction of God, Abraham sent Hagar and Ishmael into the wilderness of Beersheba:

> *So Abraham rose early in the morning, and took bread and a skin of water; and putting it on her shoulder, he gave it and the boy to Hagar, and sent her away. ...And the water in the skin was used up, and she placed the boy under one of the shrubs. Then she went and sat down across from him at a distance of about a bowshot; for she*

*said to herself, "Let me not see the death of the boy." So
she sat opposite him, and lifted up her voice and wept*
(Genesis 21:14-16).

At this point, we can look at Hagar and Ishmael and feel sorry
for them. Hagar was a single parent and Ishmael was an only son,
placed in a situation that was not of his doing. Hagar had been
given to Abraham, and Ishmael had been birthed out of an illegitimate consummation. This was not God's plan or will, but it was
the situation nonetheless.

How many single parents and children of single-parent homes
find themselves in situations that are not of their doing? They are
strapped with financial responsibilities that are impossible. They
have been sent packing or find themselves cast out of a secure
home. They have been birthed out of an illegitimate consummation and then sent away to a wilderness.

In the wilderness you run out of resources—food, water, and
shelter. Sometimes you end up with an empty water skin and a
shrinking shrub as your shelter. If you drive through the inner
cities of America, you will see a great number of Hagars and Ish-
maels. Their resources have run out. They're living in dilapidated
houses and beat-up cars. Their cupboards are bare, and their water
skins are empty.

Survival through the day is at the top of their priority list.
Single mothers are working two and three jobs so their Ishmael
won't die. Single dads are weeping over their sons and daughters
because they are providing nothing more than a shrinking shrub
for safety.

Hagar found herself in such a place. She was weeping, knowing
that her son was about to die. What was she supposed to tell her
child? What could be done to save him? Yet, what is interesting is
that Hagar was not the only one weeping. Ishmael was also crying,
because an angel of God called to Hagar from Heaven saying,

"Hagar, what's wrong? Do not be afraid! God has heard the boy crying as he lies there" (Gen. 21:17 NLT).

Sometimes parents think that they are the only ones weeping. They see their own tears without seeing the tears of their children. They empathize over their own plight without understanding the plight of their children. How many parents recognize their own need for spiritual re-formation without recognizing the need of their children? Although God heard the voice of Hagar, the Scripture clearly states that He heard the voice of Ishmael.

What a beautiful picture of the compassion of God! Oh, that the children of the world would know that God hears their cries, sees their tears, and understands their hearts. It was Ishmael's cry that turned the heart of God and inspired Him to act supernaturally.

As a parent, I sometimes worry about my own children because I know that I won't always be able to sustain them or protect them. There is no way for me to attend every concert, ball game, class, or job interview. I won't be able to protect daddy's boy or daddy's girl in every juncture of life.

Yet, there is comfort in knowing that if I can teach my children to cry out to God, He will assure me as He did Hagar, *"Do not be afraid! God has heard the boy crying as he lies there."* When I'm not there or can't be there, I can still trust in God. My personal, intimate, heavenly Father knows where he is. I may not know, but He does. He knows when he is on the back side of the desert under a shrub. He knows when he has run out of resources and needs to be comforted.

God knows about the little boy who is sleeping in the back seat of a beat-up car or the little girl who is holding an empty water skin. He knows about the little one walking around in shoes with no shoelaces. God knows, and yet He also has a part for us to play. Notice what God tells Hagar to do: *"Arise, lift up the lad and hold him with your hand, for I will make him a great nation"* (Gen. 21:18).

ARISE!

Blessing your children begins with a commitment to action—getting your lazy self off the couch, putting the remote control down, and doing something. As parents, we must not settle for inactivity.

Our American culture is waging war for the hearts and minds of our children. Billions of dollars are being spent to catch their eyes through advertisement and entertainment. Television and Hollywood purport the abnormal as normal and the extreme as "mainstream America."

A generation ago, the cultural environment was completely different. These days, music groups shout obscenities in crowded concert halls. Pornography is shown in movie halls. Condoms are distributed in high school halls, and nuclear holocaust is discussed in congressional halls.

Today, you can turn the television on at just about any time of day and select from a menu of programs sensationalizing all kinds of distorted perceptions of marriage and family. Same-sex marriage is promoted as a positive way of life when the Bible certainly does not agree. Even history shows that heterosexual marriage has been the cornerstone of every civilization from the beginning of humanity.

Of course, there have been times when homosexuality was embraced by segments of certain cultures, as it was in ancient Greece or Rome. Yet, if you spin a globe and stop it with your finger on any inhabited landmass, you can be assured that the region on which your finger rests has always embraced heterosexual marriage as the norm. No exceptions!

A study was done in the Netherlands, where gay marriage has been legal for some time. The study found that the average homosexual relationship lasted only 1.5 years, and that homosexual men had an average of eight sexual partners per year outside their "primary" relationship. Does that sound like a stable child-rearing environment? By stark contrast, 67 percent of first marriages in the United States last ten years or more, and more than 75 percent of heterosexual married couples report being faithful to their vows.[3]

The message of this study is quite clear, and yet the message that continues to be highlighted from Hollywood is that "gay is OK." The reality is that the more our culture moves toward same-sex marriage, the more the purpose of the family erodes.

Although many good educators and teachers exist in our public schools, there is such a mixture of truth with half-truth that more and more of our young people can't tell the difference between black and white, and they end up living their lives somewhere in the gray area.

I was having a conversation with a young couple in Edinburgh, Scotland. The girl had grown up in a Christian family and knew the Bible. When she first met her boyfriend, she knew it was not right for her to have sex with him. Yet, her conscience had become dull enough to tolerate the sin. After talking awhile, she finally blurted out in frustration, "Who knows what's right and wrong anymore? I don't really care." She had opted to reside in the gray area of life.

Even the Christian community can grow numb to the battle. Some Christians become tired of struggling against government bureaucracies, advertisers, the media, and corporations that really don't care about their children. Showing up at school board meetings and desiring to give input concerning what your children read and hear becomes wearisome, especially when educators seek to dismiss you as lightweights when discussing academia.

In the sociopolitical sphere, you become branded as bigoted, right-winged, fanatical, conservative, fundamentalist pigs, especially in the pro-life debate. Consequently, while some Christian parents are still getting in the ring to fight for what they believe, others have retreated to the comfort of their churches. They huddle in their comfortable little social clubs and just hope it all goes away.

Or, they have become so hardened by the violence, the killing, the teenage pregnancies, the drugs and alcohol, and the deaths and suicides that they have isolated themselves from the pain by erecting emotional walls to keep the painful stimuli from getting in.

Recently, I was talking with Ron Luce from Teen Mania and he shared the observation: "Whoever wants our kids the most in America will get them." We must not bury our heads in the sand and hope that kids will survive the spiritual onslaught against them. Just as Hagar was instructed, we must arise! We have a mission field right here under our noses, and that mission field is the family.

LIFT UP THE LAD!

Pull him out of his hole! Comfort him through his tears! Rescue him from his desperation! Ishmael is like the little boy who was separated from his mother in the mall. He was looking around for his mommy and began to cry because everyone was a stranger and he didn't know what to do. The store was packed, and everything looked so confusing. But all of a sudden, his mother found him and picked him up. His eyes began to dry, not because his surroundings changed, but because of whose arms he was in.

Have you ever read the story in Mark 9 of the distraught father who brought his demon-possessed son to Jesus's disciples for deliverance? This boy was not just troubled or rebellious; he was full of evil spirits that controlled his attitudes and actions. His situation was well-known throughout the region.

Can you image how other parents in the area responded to him? When they saw him approaching, they certainly rushed their children indoors. In all probability, he had no friends and received very little compassion; his life was hopeless.

This young man was deaf and speechless, spewing out a long barrage of guttural sounds. He foamed at the mouth like a mad dog, and he was skin and bones, emaciated from his constant struggle.

No doubt his father had to constantly hang onto him because the demons sought to kill him by casting him into the nearest river, lake, or fire.

I wonder how many times this father had to dive into a pond and drag out his son to resuscitate him, or how many burns he acquired by trying to pull his son out of a fire. We certainly consider the burns and scars the son obtained, but how many burns and scars did the father acquire? The father's heart had been broken time and time again.

If anyone could have given up and laughed at the vision of seeing his son whole, it should have been this father. He could have walked into a counseling session and said, "There is no hope for my family." In fact, he had brought his son to the disciples and asked them to heal him, but they could not. Even the scribes and religious leaders began saying, "Why is the boy not healed? Is this case too difficult for your Lord? Is the devil more powerful in this kind of situation?"

Sometimes you will not be able to answer the critics when your family is in crisis mode. You may even be disappointed with godly men and women who can't produce at the moment of your need. This father certainly felt this way. Listen to his prayer request:

> ...Teacher, I brought You my son who has a mute spirit. And wherever it seizes him, it throws him down; he foams at the mouth, gnashes his teeth, and becomes rigid. So I spoke to Your disciples, that they should cast it out, but they could not. ...And often he has thrown him both into the fire and into the water to destroy him. But if You can do anything, have compassion on us and help us (Mark 9:17-18,22).

Jesus responded by saying: "If you can believe, all things are possible to him who believes" (Mark 9:23). With these powerful words, Jesus gazed through the corridor of time right into the 21st century

to ask us: "Do you believe I can handle your hopeless situation? Do you believe I can heal your burned and scarred son? Do you believe I can take a hopeless home and re-form it?"

There is no situation too hopeless for God. Burns and scars are not too difficult for Him. With one word, Jesus changed the impossible into the possible for the boy and his father: *"Deaf and dumb spirit, I command you, come out of him and enter him no more!"* (Mark 9:25).

Can you imagine the joy that occurred at that moment? Can you imagine the boy set free, settling into his father's embrace?

HOLD HIM WITH YOUR HAND!

Hug him! Embrace him! Show Ishmael that he is valued. Ishmael had been birthed from an illegitimate consummation. He represented the failure of Abraham's faith. He had been ostracized and sent away from Abraham's house. Yet, when Hagar lifted him up and held him with her hand, she blessed him and told him what God had said about him, "I will make him a great nation."

God sees so much more than we may see. We may see a snotty, dirty-faced kid, but God sees a nation. We may see a helpless, hopeless child, but God sees a destiny. When we view a child, we may not see much, but God sees spiritual re-formation. God sees the potential of every child and the ability to change the destinies of families and generations to come.

Ever since my sons were toddlers I have tried to instill within them that they would become godly men who make a worldwide difference. I have prayed it over them and spoken it over them in faith. Although I have never pressured them to enter into the full-time ministry, I have always encouraged them to be godly men who make a difference for Christ.

My middle son, Garrett, has often talked about serving as a children's pastor or youth pastor. He is certainly not reserved in communicating his passion to serve in the fivefold ministry. When he was 11 years old, I took him on a mission trip down the Amazon River in Brazil, and he preached his first sermon to a crowd of 300 people. At the close of the message, he called for people to come forward, and he prayed for them at the altar. His commitment to ministry has been evident from a young age.

However, my oldest son, Spencer, had always offered very little information concerning ministry as he grew up. In fact, he is an excellent athlete and continued to express an interest in playing collegiate baseball. I remember visiting one particular Bible college, and when the admissions counselor asked his area of interest, his response included playing baseball and nothing else.

But I will never forget the night when he followed me into my bedroom with tears streaming down his face. He said, "Dad, I need to tell you something. A couple of weeks ago at youth camp, the Lord spoke to me for the first time. He told me that baseball should not be my priority, because I am called into full-time ministry."

For my teenage son, who had seldom expressed interest in following in his dad's footsteps, the light had been turned on. He had experienced a spiritual re-formation moment, and I was able to bless him and say, "The same God who spoke to you for the first time will make of you a great nation."

Could God have blessed Ishmael without Hagar? Absolutely! Yet, in this instance God used Hagar's hand—"*hold him with your hand.*" He used Hagar to bring supernatural blessing:

> *Then God opened her eyes, and she saw a well of water. And she went and filled the skin with water, and gave the lad a drink* (Genesis 21:19).

Sometimes we expect God to do all of the work by Himself, but in this instance, Ishmael's blessing was dependent upon his mother, Hagar. Perhaps we should say it this way: "If we will arise, God will open our eyes." If we will get busy blessing our kids, God

will get busy providing supernatural solutions! He will provide a well of water that we didn't see the first time. He will enter into a sacred cooperation with us to bring about His desired end. Listen to the testimony of Ishmael's life:

> *So God was with the lad; and he grew and dwelt in the wilderness, and became an archer. He dwelt in the Wilderness of Paran; and his mother took a wife for him from the land of Egypt* (Genesis 21:20-21).

Ishmael prospered in the very place where he expected to die. He succeeded in the wilderness and became a warrior. God loves to do that for His kids. He will save them from the wilderness to prosper them in the wilderness. He'll deliver them from the ghetto so they can prosper in the ghetto. He'll pull them out of a broken family so they can bless other broken families. Ishmael became a great example of how God will turn our circumstances into blessings.

RE-FORMATION CHALLENGE

The British poet Michael Roberts said, "How can I teach, how can I save this child whose features are my own, who feet run down the way that I have walked."[4] The Bible provides the answer: *"The righteous man walks in his integrity; his children are blessed after him"* (Prov. 20:7).

There is a cloud of blessing that hovers over a family where a righteous man or woman is communicating a positive picture of God, marriage and family, and faith.

In fact, God created man and woman to reflect who He is: *"So God created man in his own image; in the image of God He created him; male and female He created them"* (Gen. 1:27).

Have you thought about the powerful truth that you have the opportunity to reflect the manifest image of God? When you walk into a restaurant, board an airplane, or walk down the street, someone can say, "There goes the image of God." Literally, you can become the manifest image of God to the world.

Now take this truth to the next level, because God is not only interested in your reflection of who He is, but He is interested in your children's reflection of who He is. Adam and Eve were created to multiply: *"Then God blessed them, and God said to them, 'Be fruitful and multiply...'"* (Gen. 1:28).

Despite what some parents think, having children is a blessing and not a curse. When we have children, we have the opportunity to multiply the blessing. If our children experience spiritual re-formation, we can multiply the manifest image of God wherever they may go.

If your child moves to New York and reflects the image of God, the image of God will be multiplied in New York. If your child moves overseas to Africa and reflects the image of God, the image of God will be multiplied in Africa. The very reason God created marriage and family was to multiply and reflect who He is to the world!

So, what do we tell our kids? We tell them they are the manifest image of God. We affirm them and let them know that God stamped His image on them, and because of it, they can become godly men and women who make a worldwide difference. We tell them that God has a design and destiny for their lives if they will follow Him.

Perhaps we should hear the words of the "great philosopher" Sydney Bristow from the television show *Alias*. Two years of her life had passed by in a state of amnesia. When she finally comes to her senses, her dad is now in prison, and her mother is presumed dead. Frustrated by what has happened, she looks up at the man of her dreams, who is now married to another woman, and says, "Vaughn, I didn't need rational answers from you; I needed faith."

That's where many of our children are living right now! They don't need all of our rational answers to life. They need us to tell them that we have faith in them. They need us to believe in them and bless them. In an age where sports heroes like Kobe Bryant and others are disappointing them, they need some moms and dads and uncles and aunts to come alongside of them and say, "God will make of you a great nation." For re-formation in our homes to occur, this is what we really need to tell our kids!

RE-FORMATION PRAYER

Heavenly Father, I pray that Your Kingdom will come and Your will be done in my family. I ask that You pull my kids and family members out of the fire and make them whole again. I beseech You to speak the word so that they will be healed. With Your help, I will become a conduit of Your blessing. With Your help, I will arise and lift them up. With Your help, I will hold them with my hand and speak faith concerning their destinies. With Your help, I will open up the lines of communication to coach and mentor them. With Your help, I will reflect Your manifest image to them so that they can do the same to their world. I pray these things in Jesus's name, amen.

RE-FORMATION BUILDERS

Personal Evaluation

In the example of Ishmael, God demonstrates how much He loves our children. Ishmael was not the son of promise; yet God sustained him and blessed him. Allow the lessons learned through Hagar and Ishmael to help you evaluate your responsibility to your own family.

1. What were the positive truths that stood out to you in the way God treated Hagar and Ishmael?

2. If God is willing to take care of Hagar and Ishmael, what does this say about His willingness to take care of your family?

3. Are your kids in crisis mode? If so, what are some specific ways to partner with God for their spiritual re-formation?

4. Have you thought about the fact that you are the reflection of God to your children and the world? If so, what attitudes and actions need to change to provide a positive reflection of God?

5. What do you specifically need to tell your kids that will build their self-esteem and bless them?

Group Discussion

In the example of Ishmael, God demonstrates how much He loves our children. Ishmael was not the son of promise; yet God sustained him and blessed him. Allow the lessons learned through Hagar and Ishmael to help you discuss the responsibility that you have to your own family.

1. Discuss the statement, "Whoever wants our kids the most will have them."

2. Because of television and social networking, very few subjects are now off-limits. Discuss specific ways to open up the lines of communication with the younger generation.

3. In an age when superstars and athletes are catching the eye of America's children, discuss practical ways to bring about a proper balance in the way they view them.

4. Have you ever been disappointed with the way godly men and women have responded to you in family crises? If so, discuss proper ways to respond that will be life-giving.

5. God entered into a sacred cooperation with Hagar to bring about the best for Ishmael. Discuss the biblical principle of "sacred cooperation" and your participation in it.

ENDNOTES

1. Ravi Zacharias, *The Grand Weaver* (Grand Rapids, MI: Zondervan, 2007), 53.

2. The Bloodhound Gang, "The Bad Touch," in *Hooray for Boobies*, Interscope Records, 2000, accessed February 5, 2011, http://www. metrolyrics.com/the-bad-touch-lyrics-bloodhound-gang.html.

3. "The Contribution of Steady and Casual Partnerships to the Incidence of HIV Infection Among Homosexual Men in Amsterdam," *AIDS* 17, no. 7 (May 2, 2003): 1029.

4. Michael Roberts, *The Faber Book of Modern Verse* (London: Faber and Faber, 1936).

SECTION THREE

RE>FORMING YOUR HOPE!

CHAPTER SEVEN

MAXIMIZING GOD LESSONS

> Biblical Challenge—THE 22-YEAR DREAM

> Biblical Example—JOSEPH

Now Joseph had a dream, and he told it to his brothers; and they hated him even more (Genesis 37:5).

One of the most telling tales of re-formation is found in the life of Joseph. Joseph had a dream when he was 17, but for 22 years God took him through a spiritual marathon of re-forming his hope. God often does the same for us.

God has some plans for us! In fact, notice what He says in Jeremiah:

> *"For I know the plans I have for you," says the Lord. "They are plans for good and not for disaster, to give you a **future** and a **hope**"* (Jeremiah 29:11 NLT).

Isn't it interesting that the word *future* is listed before the word *hope?* I believe that God states it this way because seeing your

future is directly linked to re-forming your hope. When you are seeing something, you are conceiving something. When you are seeing a future, you are conceiving hope.

The reason why some people begin losing their hope is because they stop seeing their future. They stop dreaming dreams. There is even a physiological process that is in play here! Solomon said, *"Hope deferred makes the heart sick"* (Prov. 13:12).

How do you end up with a sick heart? You lose your hope! How is your hope deferred or displaced? You lose your future. Notice the progression—a sick heart results from deferred hope, which is produced by losing your future. In other words, your hope is dependent upon seeing your future and dreaming dreams.

Many Christians engage in what I like to call the "22-Year Dream"—a dream marathon that unfolds every day of their lives. They begin down a path of dreaming dreams. They have dreams for themselves, their families, their businesses, or their churches, but their dreams seem to take forever to fulfill.

The only people who aren't dreaming dreams are "the dead"—those who are dead in the grave or dead on the inside. Sometimes dreams can become devalued or displaced when people give up on them. At other times, dreams may change with the seasons of life. Yet, deep in the heart of every man and woman there are dreams still stirring and declaring, "I'm still here. Don't forget about me. I'm too important to lose."

God made a profound statement in Acts:

> *And it shall come to pass in the last days, says God, that I will pour out of My Spirit on all flesh; your sons and your daughters shall prophesy, your young men shall see visions, your old men shall dream dreams* (Acts 2:17).

The neon sign that God's Spirit is being poured out today is that our sons and daughters are prophesying or declaring the dreams and plans of God; our young men will see visions, and our old men will dream dreams. Dreaming dreams is an evidential sign that God is at work in the midst of His people.

Most of the time, you begin with a dream. You dream something from a distance. Yet, the dream remains a dream until you envision how to accomplish it. A dream is "what you sleep on," while a vision is "what you act on." A dream is something you hope will happen, while a vision is something you seek to accomplish. A dreamer will end up hoping, while a visionary will end up facilitating.

This is why those who are older in age tend to dream more dreams, and those who are younger in age tend to see more visions. Those who are older move into seasons of time when they are less likely to engage their dreams. Those who are older will dream dreams and hope that their dreams will come true, while those who are younger will see visions and act upon what they see.

Consequently, the older and the younger need each other. The older need the younger to help them engage their dreams, and the younger need the older to make sure that their visions stay on track. Is it possible that some people don't have the right visions because they don't have the right dreams? If dreaming dreams becomes a catalyst for visions, then having the right dreams is paramount to realizing the right visions.

Joseph had a dream from the Lord that his father and brothers would bow before him. He said:

> *"There we were, binding sheaves in the field. Then behold, my sheaf arose and stood upright; and indeed your sheaves stood all around and bowed down to my sheaf." And his brothers said to him, "Shall you indeed reign over us? Or shall you indeed have dominion over us?" So they*

hated him even more for his dreams and for his words
(Genesis 37:7-8).

Now, that's not the kind of dream that would cause you to pump your fist with glee. God doesn't always give you fist-pumping dreams. God will give you functional dreams—dreams that are filled with His purpose! He will provide dreams that fulfill His plan and impact eternity.

Joseph's dream wasn't a "grab it and blab it" dream—one that you share with the world. Yet, that's what Joseph did anyway. He blabbed his dream to his brothers, and his brothers grabbed him and despised him for it.

Before we judge Joseph too harshly, Joseph's dream was still given by God. Perhaps Joseph's father and brothers needed to hear it so God could eventually prove that it was true. Whether sharing his dream was a mistake or not, Joseph was at the beginning of a "22-Year Dream."

Joseph began to experience a time of preparation that would help him serve others effectively. Preparation is not so painful when you consciously choose it. What causes preparation to become painful is when you keep learning the same God-lesson over and over again because you don't maximize the lesson the first time. When we go through a God-lesson, nothing should be more encouraging than knowing that God isn't mocking us, but He is preparing us for the task ahead. He is shaping us for success and re-forming our hope.

Unfortunately for Joseph, his lesson began with betrayal from his brothers.

> *Then they said to one another, "Look, this dreamer is coming! Come therefore, let us now kill him and cast him into some pit; and we shall say, 'Some wild beast has devoured him.' We shall see what will become of his dreams!"* (Genesis 37:19-20)

LESSON I:
OVERCOMING THE DREAM-TAKERS—
TRUSTING GOD IN THE PIT!

Whenever you are a dreamer, you will encounter the scoffers behind closed doors who will say, "We shall see what will become of his dreams." The cynical love to say, "Look, here comes the dreamer. Here comes the guy who is a few cards short of a full deck or a few bricks short of a full load!" These people are dream-takers. They attempt to keep you in the pit of hopelessness.

Dream-Takers

Dream-takers are "the glass is half empty" people. They would rather criticize you than encourage you. When they look at you, they see the deficiencies in themselves. They become jealous of your dreams, and they despise their own lack of faith and vision.

Because they are not happy with what they have, they want to take what you've received. They say, "Why has he received a coat of many colors?" Insecurities seek to destroy them, so their only solace is to try and steal your coat until they feel good about themselves.

Joseph's brothers were dream-takers—coat-stealers! When they saw Joseph coming from a distance, they began to scoff at him and conspire against him: "Look, here comes the dreamer. Look at the way he dresses. Look at the way he walks and talks. He is so full of himself."

Dream-takers will conspire against you "before" you come near: "How can we downsize this dreamer? How can we teach him a lesson?" The reality is that they're not really trying to kill you; they're trying to kill your dreams. "Let's see what will become of his dreams."

The problem with the dream-takers is that they are messing with their blessing. As long as Noah remains on board the boat, the boat will float. As long as Moses talks to God, manna keeps

showing up. As long as Joshua leads the Israelites into battle, the people possess the land. As long as David is king, the Philistines bow their knee in defeat. As long as Esther is queen, the nation is saved.

So, why do dream-takers get so bent out of shape because God makes a shepherd boy a king, chooses Mary to be the mother of the Messiah, or gives their brother a coat of many colors to bless his ministry? When God blesses others, He is ultimately blessing them. Wouldn't serving others become more effective if we had more dream-makers than dream-takers?

Dream-Makers

What would serving others look like if we could get a few more people who would make our dreams rather than take our dreams? Cain, who killed his brother Abel, asked God the question, *"Am I my brother's keeper?"* (Gen. 4:9). Shouldn't we be a part of keeping our brother's dream on course until it comes true?

Sometimes people who are outside the Church seem to be better dream-makers than those inside the Church. Pharaoh was a heathen king, and he believed in Joseph more than Joseph's own family believed in him. Imagine Pharaoh taking Joseph, a convict in prison, seriously. Can you hear Pharaoh's advisors: "Do you realize who you are listening to here? You are listening to a criminal and a convicted rapist, who is a foreigner." In fact, Joseph had earlier shared an interpretation of Pharaoh's dream that would take another 14 years to prove—7 years of plenty and 7 years of famine.

Yet, Pharaoh had such confidence in Joseph that he made the following observation: *"Isn't this the man we need? Are we going to find anyone else who has God's Spirit in him like this?"* (Gen. 41:38 MSG). Pharaoh believed in Joseph's dream, and he believed in the Spirit of God that was in Joseph.

The reality is that you may not always know your leaders personally or be intimately connected to their lives, but do you recognize the Spirit of God in them? Are their steps ordered by the Lord? You may say, "But how can I really know?" In Pharaoh's situation, Joseph not only gave an explanation of the dream, but he also gave an application of the dream. Some people can dream dreams and explain them, but can they dream dreams and provide application? God tends to hang out with the doers of the dreams, not just the hearers of the dreams.

So, Pharaoh plays the role of a dream-maker. Here is the man who holds the greatest power in that era, humbling himself and listening to a slave and a convict. Yet, Joseph had to maximize some God-lessons to get to this point of elevation.

LESSON 2:
SERVING ANOTHER MAN'S HOUSE—
TRUSTING GOD OFF THE PEDESTAL!

After Joseph was betrayed by his brothers, he found a brief respite in the house of Potiphar in Egypt. In fact, the Bible says:

> *His master saw that the Lord was with him and that the Lord made all he did to prosper in his hand. ...Then he made him overseer of his house, and all that he had he put under his authority* (Genesis 39:3-4).

Joseph was so blessed by the Lord that he soon found himself on a pedestal of prestige in Potiphar's house. Everything that he touched was blessed, and Potiphar trusted Joseph with everything in his house. However, Potiphar's wife soon desired Joseph, and she began to make overtures toward him repeatedly. But Joseph denied her advances because he was faithful to his master. He chose to serve and protect his master's house even though he was falsely accused and thrust into prison.

Can you imagine what Joseph must have thought when he ended up in prison unjustly? He had been betrayed by his own

brothers and thrown into a pit, and now after serving his master's house faithfully, he found himself in prison for a crime he didn't commit.

I'll never forget visiting a prison in Wolayita Soddo, Ethiopia, to speak to a group of prisoners. While there, I met a young prisoner who was serving as the primary pastor to the Christian men in that prison. As we spent time together, he shared the tragic story of how his wife had been murdered and how he had been falsely accused and condemned to a life sentence without parole. What was deeply humbling to me was the fact that he expressed no frustration in this tragic event whatsoever. In fact, he rejoiced in the opportunity that God had provided for him to pastor those men in prison. He had allowed God to re-form his hope.

In many ways, this is how I believe Joseph responded to being knocked off his pedestal at Potiphar's house. He was falsely accused, and yet I believe Joseph maximized his God-lesson. He behaved himself in a decent and honorable way when fleeing from sexual temptation, and he no doubt behaved in a God-pleasing way concerning his plight in prison. We read:

> *The Lord was with Joseph and showed him mercy, and He gave him favor in the sight of the keeper of the prison. And the keeper of the prison committed to Joseph's hand all the prisoners who were in the prison; whatever they did there, it was his doing* (Genesis 39:21-22).

LESSONS 3:
TWO MORE YEARS—TRUSTING GOD IN THE PRISON!

Joseph had gone through the pit—the betrayal of his brothers—and he experienced getting knocked off the pedestal—the false accusations of Potiphar's wife. Now, Joseph wound up in prison, and even though God blessed him, Joseph had to endure his greatest test of trusting God. How do you hold onto your dreams at a dead-end street? How do you keep dreaming dreams in a dungeon?

Have you ever considered that sometimes the dream-takers in your life are not people but circumstances? Now you are older, or your health is not as good. Perhaps you haven't finished your education, or your financial condition is restrictive. How can your dream come true when your circumstances have changed?

Joseph must have felt that way in prison, and yet Joseph's story reveals that dead-end streets can become opportunities for new streets to be constructed with God. While in prison, Joseph was placed in a position to interpret the dreams of Pharaoh's butler and baker. He told the butler that he would be reinstated to his royal position, but he told the baker that he wouldn't be so blessed. However, what is interesting is what Joseph said to the butler before his reinstatement:

> But remember me when it is well with you, and please show kindness to me; make mention of me to Pharaoh, and get me out of this house (Genesis 40:14).

At the outset, Joseph's request doesn't sound bad at all. He simply seems to be asking for help from a friend. Yet, there is a deeper issue at work here. Joseph was trying to find a way out of jail on his own rather than depending on God.

All of us have acted just like Joseph—seeking to find a way out of our situation without God. We have a dream, but rather than waiting on God, we take matters into our own hands.

Henry Blackaby, who wrote the wonderful book *Spiritual Leadership*, tells of a man who approached him one day at a large convention. The distinguished middle-aged man had been a pastor at some point, but he had left the pastorate to become a vice president of a newly formed company. The company experienced enormous

success and made him a wealthy and respected administrative vice president.

However, as the man began to recount the story of how God had re-formed him through a discipleship course at his church, he was suddenly overcome with emotion. With his voice breaking, he recalled, "God got a hold of me!" As he turned to go, he smiled, and through his tears, he said, "I'm a pastor again!"[1] Who among us does not leave God behind at times, even though it may not be a purposeful slight?

Now, you might think that God should have given Joseph some latitude. After all, Joseph had experienced betrayal in the pit and persecution on the pedestal. Now he is serving an unjust prison sentence for a wrong he didn't even commit. Perhaps Joseph threw up his hands more than once and said, "Please, God, work with me here." Yet, God was working with Joseph in ways that were necessary for Joseph's success, even if he didn't realize it. He was working on Joseph's dependency issues.

Joseph was still hanging on to the thread of his own ability to save himself because he continues to say to the butler:

> For indeed I was stolen away from the land of the Hebrews; and also I have done nothing here that they should put me into the dungeon (Genesis 40:15).

After all the great strides Joseph had made toward spiritual re-formation in serving God, he defended himself and his actions.

Unfortunately, too many people grasp at the idea that their religious faith is simply based on what they have or have not done. One afternoon, I was flying from San Francisco to Memphis, and I sat next to a young woman from India. The topic of religion came up in the conversation, and her religion of choice was Jainism—a particular sect of Hinduism. She shared, "I am a vegetarian, and I don't eat meat or anything that grows below the ground."

After a long explanation of the litany of rules and regulations that she adhered to on a daily basis, I asked her, "It sounds like you give quite a bit to your religion. Does your religion give anything back to you?"

She looked perplexed, and after quite a pause, she said, "I don't know." Thankfully, many of us have a different answer. Our God has given us more than we could ever give back to Him, and His giving nature is manifested daily as we depend upon Him.

Now, God could have used Joseph's reminder to the butler to save him, and Joseph could have "chalked one up to God" saying, "Look how God brought me out of this prison." And yet, God still had His own *modus operandi*—He would exalt Joseph without Joseph's help.

So the butler was restored to his original position, while Joseph was a forgotten man. Joseph still had to endure the prison for two more years. Notice what happened: *"Yet the chief butler did not remember Joseph, but forgot him. Then it came to pass, at the end of two full years"* (Gen. 40:23–41:1).

What is the lesson to be learned here? The self-promoters and self-politicians get two more years in prison. They can't promote themselves or play their get-out-of-jail-free cards. They just have to go through two more years! One may say, "But what if I know my destiny, and I know God's will?" Sometimes, your knowledge is incomplete.

Moses thought that it was God's will for him to lead the people into the Promised Land, but Moses didn't receive that opportunity. David thought it was God's will for him to build a temple dedicated to God, but he was sadly mistaken. The only one who knows the end from the beginning is God (see Isa. 46:10).

God is the only one who knows what will happen two minutes from now or two years from now. He knew the exact day when your earthly existence would begin, and He knows the exact day when it will end.

Those who believe that they have God all figured out spend two more years in the prison of their dead-end circumstances. The job promotion that has been promised isn't offered. The financial windfall that is just around the corner never comes. The ministry that has been prophesied is no closer today than it was yesterday. So how should we approach God's partnership with our dreams?

THE "BUT IF NOT" HOPE

The three Hebrew children who were facing life and death before a fiery furnace certainly help us here:

> *...Our God whom we serve is able to deliver us from the burning fiery furnace, and he will deliver us from your hand, O king. But if not, let it be known to you, O king, that we do not serve your gods...* (Daniel 3:17-18).

Shadrach, Meshach, and Abednego teach us the "divine sovereignty" stage of hope, which is serving God whether He chooses to save us from the fiery furnace or not.

In Joseph's situation, Joseph was learning to serve God whether he was free from the prison or not. When you maximize this God-lesson, you know that the God you serve is able to fulfill your dream, but if not, you will serve Him anyway.

THE "LACKING NOTHING" HOPE

James declares, *"But let patience have its perfect work, that you may be perfect and complete, lacking nothing"* (James 1:4).

Joseph was learning to experience two more years of lacking nothing in character and integrity and preparation. The "lacking nothing" hope is the "spiritual maturity" stage of hope.

Warren Bennis observed: "Leaders, like anyone else, are the sum of all their experiences, but, unlike others, they amount to more than the sum, because they make more of their experiences."[2] In other words, experience is not an end, but a means to develop maturity for effective leadership.

Is it possible that you aren't possessing the land because you still need some preparation? When the children of Israel were liberated from Egypt, they could not possess the Promised Land because they were still Egyptian slaves in their minds. How many people are not out of prison yet because they still possess a prisoner's mindset? If you are not a king yet, you may not be ready to be crowned, and you may still need two more years of lacking nothing in leadership.

THE "LEARNING CONTENTMENT" HOPE

The apostle Paul said, *"Not that I speak in regard to need, for I have learned in whatever state I am, to be content"* (Phil. 4:11). The "learning contentment" hope is the "fleshly crucifixion" stage of hope. You learn to crucify your flesh with its affections and lusts in order to please the Lord.

What if God chooses not to fulfill your dream? Just like Moses, what if He allows you to wander around for 40 years and you never get there? Will you still be content? Will you still be able to say, "I have learned in whatever state I am to be content"?

Notice the three phases of the "two more years" part of the dream:

1) "But if not"—Divine Sovereignty (dependence upon God)

2) "Lacking nothing"—Spiritual Maturity (development of character)

3) "Learning contentment"—Fleshly Crucifixion (death to self)

This is what you must go through to maximize the "two more years" stage of dreaming. You must go through two more years of learning God's sovereignty, two more years of learning spiritual maturity, and two more years of learning fleshly crucifixion!

But if you can pass the class, God may choose to give you your diploma with a quick graduation. All of a sudden, you may be standing in front of the king, just like Joseph, doing what you do best—wearing the king's robe, holding the king's crown, and using the king's ring as a sacred seal of your coronation! After 13 years of sorrow, Joseph was elevated to the palace at 30 years of age.

LESSON 4:
LEARNING THE FAMILY
SECRET—TRUSTING GOD IN THE PALACE!

The challenging part of the "22-Year Dream" is that you never see the total picture until you get there. When Joseph was a 17-year-old boy, he only saw the dream from a distance. But later on in the palace, he saw the big picture and told his brothers:

> ...I am Joseph your brother, whom you sold into Egypt. But now, do not therefore be grieved or angry with your-selves because you sold me here; for God sent me before you to preserve life. ...And God sent me before you to preserve a posterity for you in the earth, and to save your lives by a great deliverance (Genesis 45:4-5,7).

Joseph declared that God had sent him to Egypt to preserve his brothers and their families. The dream was not really about his father (representing the previous generation) bowing down before him, or his brothers (representing the present generation) bowing down before him. The dream was about saving his brothers' posterity, which represented the next generation. The essence of the dream involved a remnant, not rulership.

How many people are captivated by rulership rather than a remnant? They are passionate about a position when God is passionate about a possession—possessing the next generation. Our dreams are not really about us; our dreams are about the next generation. God took Noah on a 120-year boat-building marathon to preserve the next generation. God took Abraham on a 25-year star-gazing tour to preserve the next generation. God took Moses on a 40-year wilderness excursion to preserve the next generation! God will preserve the next generation through our dreams and visions.

Joseph went on to say to his brothers:

> *So now it was not you who sent me here, but God; and He has made me a father to Pharaoh, and lord of all his house, and a ruler throughout all the land of Egypt* (Genesis 45:8).

Imagine that! Joseph, a 30-year-old young man, is now the father to Pharaoh! He is the father figure to the most powerful man on the planet.

Joseph's dream as a teenager hadn't revealed that aspect. He saw his father and brothers bowing before him, but not the most prestigious man on the planet. Have you learned the family secret yet? Your dream doesn't even compare to God's dream! What you see isn't even comparable with what He sees! You see the small picture, but He sees the big picture. You see rulership, but He sees a remnant! You see yourself, but He sees the next generation. You see fame and fortune, but He sees your fatherhood over Pharaoh.

RE-FORMATION CHALLENGE

Now, let's return to the dream that Joseph shared with his brothers in the beginning:

There we were, binding sheaves in the field. Then behold, my sheaf arose and stood upright; and indeed your sheaves stood all around and bowed down to my sheaf. And his brothers said to him, "Shall you indeed reign over us? Or shall you indeed have dominion over us?" So they hated him even more for his dreams and for his words (Genesis 37:7-8).

Joseph didn't realize that it would take 22 years for his dream to come true—13 years until his reign under Pharaoh, then 7 years of ruling during the 7 years of plenty, and 2 years of ruling during the famine before his brother's bowed before him.

However, whether your dream takes 22 years or 44 years, God can re-form your hope so that you will trust Him whether your dream comes true or not. You won't burn out because you go through decades of humbling experiences before you fulfill your destiny.

God orders your steps. If you have connected with the Author and the Finisher of your faith, you can become confident of this very thing—*"that He who has begun a good work in you will complete it until the day of Jesus Christ"* (Phil. 1:6).

RE-FORMATION PRAYER

Heavenly Father, help me to maximize the God-lessons in my life. When I go through my own version of the pit, the pedestal, the prison, and the palace, teach me to follow in Your steps. Stir up the dreams that You have birthed inside of me and identify those people in my life who will be dream-makers and not dream-takers. Oh God, provide the grace to help me overcome all attempts to shortcut Your preparation process in my "22-year dream." I will trust You to fulfill it, but if not, I will trust You anyway. I will learn how to lack nothing, and I will learn to have contentment in all things. Oh God, I have learned the family secret—the posterity of the next generation is far more important than anything I might see. Oh God, I submit to Your will and Your way in Jesus's name, amen.

RE-FORMATION BUILDERS

Personal Evaluation

Through the life of Joseph, he experiences a pit, pedestal, prison, and palace before God fulfills his "22-Year Dream." Allow the lessons learned through Joseph's life to help you maximize the God-lessons in your own life and re-form your hope.

1. Dreaming dreams is a neon sign of God's Spirit working in your life. Write out some of the dreams that you believe have been given to you by God.

2. List the obstacles that have kept you from seeing the fulfillment of your God-dreams.

3. Identify the dream-makers and the dream-takers in your life and seek God concerning your relationship with them.

4. Identify the current circumstance that you are in that relate to the pit, pedestal, prison, or palace.

5. List the lessons you have learned from Joseph that will help you through your current circumstance.

Group Discussion

Through the life of Joseph, he experiences a pit, pedestal, "22-Year Dream." Allow the lessons learned through Joseph's life to help you explore the importance of maximizing the God-lessons in your life and re-form your hope.

1. Discuss Acts 2:17 and how dreaming relates to the moving of God's Spirit.

2. Discuss the differences between dream-makers and dream-takers.

3. Allow members of the group to identify current circumstances that relate to the pit, pedestal, prison, or palace.

4. What does the term the "22-Year Dream" mean to you? Discuss some ways that people try to shortcut the "22-Year Dream" process.

5. Discuss the following:
    The "But If Not" Hope (dependence upon God)
    The "Lacking Nothing" Hope (development of character)
    The "Learning Contentment" Hope (death to self)

ENDNOTES

1. Henry Blackaby and Richard Blackaby, *Spiritual Leadership* (Nashville, TN: Broadman and Holman Publishers, 2001), 249.

2. Warren Bennis and Burt Nanus, *Leaders: Strategies for Taking Charge* (New York: HarperCollins, 1997), 40.

CHAPTER EIGHT

MINIMIZING PERSONAL AGENDAS

> Biblical Challenge—LIVING FOR AN AUDIENCE OF ONE

> Biblical Example—MOSES

By faith Moses, when he became of age, refused to be called the son of Pharaoh's daughter, choosing rather to suffer affliction with the people of God than to enjoy the passing pleasures of sin, esteeming the reproach of Christ greater riches than the treasures in Egypt; for he looked to the reward (Hebrews 11:24-26).

Life is filled with competing agendas, and the Christian life is no different. Some people follow Christ as a matter of convenience, allowing other priorities to maximize their time and energy. Are they Christians because He is first in their lives? Or are they Christians because it is the popular thing to do?

If people become Christians because of popularity, Christ becomes little more than an American flag—everyone has Him.

He is relegated to the backseat for whatever they place in the front seat of their priority list. He turns into little more than a symbol—a bumper sticker on a car or a t-shirt worn on the weekend. As long as He is only a symbol, they can pray over their food because people are watching and still live any way they choose. Their personal agendas become far more important than their relationship with Christ.

In September of 2010, I spent two hours sharing my faith with a group of atheists and agnostics called the Joplin Free Thinkers. At least there was no pretension. They did not pretend to be anyone they were not. Many of them simply did not believe in experiential truth. If God could not be seen in a test tube, He did not exist. However, the argument that faith was merely a crutch rang hollow in their halls of debate when I explained that non-faith was more of a crutch than faith.

The truth is that having no faith does not cost a thing, because you can live without any strings attached. Without faith, you have the crutch of not having to change your life. However, as soon as you put your faith in God, it costs you something. Actually, it costs you everything. Now you must live as God chooses and wills. You no longer can pretentiously pray over your food and live any way you so choose, because God expects your will to align with His Word.

The real question of authentic faith in God becomes, "Who are you living for?" or perhaps the question behind the question, "Who is your audience?" Moses was forced to address the same issue when he grew up in the house of Pharaoh. He reached a point of decision-making that would affect the rest of his life—who would he serve?

For Moses, the decision was difficult because he had to choose whether he would be associated with the people of God, who were literally slaves to the Egyptians, or the family of Pharaoh in the king's palace. He chose the people of God, even though it meant affliction and persecution.

I wonder how many of us would make that same choice. If on the one side was an invitation to become part of Hollywood's family and become the next big movie star or celebrity, and on the other side was God's family, which meant affliction and persecution as a slave, would we choose suffering with Christ or the fame and fortune of Hollywood?

The decision is certainly not an easy one, because some people seem to be making the wrong decision. They're all wrapped up in their personal agendas, seeking to find fulfillment in all the wrong places—fame, fortune, ambition, material possessions, prestige, and power! The list goes on and on.

What's the problem? People are living for the wrong audience. They are more interested in the masses, their peers, and even themselves than in serving God. Let me ask you a question that could become a catalyst for re-forming your hope—who are you living for?

WHO ARE YOU LIVING FOR?

Are you living for yourself, for others, or for God? The answer to this question will catalyze your hope more than any other. Politicians want their names to be remembered in the history books. Athletes want their names to be remembered in the record books. Men and women in business want their names to be remembered for their economic achievements. Even preachers can become more interested in their spiritual legacy than in serving people.

Allow me to introduce the life-changing principle of learning to live for an audience of One! When I refer to One, I am not referring to you. If you live for yourself, you separate yourself from God. The apostle Paul said it this way:

> *Don't be misled: No one makes a fool of God. What a person plants, he will harvest. The person who plants*

selfishness, ignoring the needs of others—ignoring God!—harvests a crop of weeds. All he'll have to show for his life is weeds! But the one who plants in response to God, letting God's Spirit do the growth work in him, harvests a crop of real life, eternal life (Galatians 6:7-8 MSG).

What is at stake is the difference between a crop of weeds and a harvest of life. Sowing to your flesh will produce selfishness, ignoring the needs of others and God's plans for your life, but sowing in God's Spirit will produce a harvest of abundant and eternal life.

Moses chose to plant for the right harvest and *"refused to be called the son of Pharaoh's daughter,"* but many people go ahead and choose the name of Pharaoh's daughter (Heb. 11:24). They enjoy living as sons of prestige and power, sons of money and materialism, sons of peer pressure and social acceptance, or even sons of the Church and religion.

Candidly, for a short time I became a son of the Church. I was a pastor who was living for a church rather than for God, and I allowed myself to become bound with religious ceremony. However, I kept hearing Christ ask the question, "Who are you living for?" I soon discovered that religion couldn't save me, but relationship with Christ could save me.

Moses had to answer the same question, and in the beginning he was living for the wrong audience. He thought his audience was Hebrew or Egyptian. Moses had been raised as an Egyptian prince, but he was really a Hebrew deliverer, which he realized when he killed an Egyptian who was mistreating a Hebrew.

In his heart he could not stand by and watch the cultural war in his community continue without entering the fray, especially when he had the influence and leadership skill to make a difference. Yet, he tried to do the right thing in the wrong way, and when his Hebrew brethren disapproved of his actions against the

Egyptian, Moses lost his way and ended up in a desert far away from his destiny.

Only a burning bush encounter with God would take him off the shelf and back into the action.

> *And the Angel of the Lord appeared to him in a flame of fire from the midst of a bush. So he looked, and behold, the bush was burning with fire, but the bush was not consumed* (Exodus 3:2).

God was getting ready to minimize Moses's agenda in the desert and initiate His own agenda for His people. Moses was getting ready to experience a God moment that would change everything. God showed up and said:

> *Now therefore, behold, the cry of the children of Israel has come to Me, and I have also seen the oppression with which the Egyptians oppress them. Come now, therefore, and I will send you to Pharaoh that you may bring My people, the children of Israel, out of Egypt* (Exodus 3:9-10).

Moses, who is a second-chance man, gets a second-chance opportunity in service. However, Moses is still conflicted by his identity crisis and says:

> *But why me? What makes You think that I could ever go to the Pharaoh and lead the children of Israel out of Egypt?* (Exodus 3:11 MSG)

A conflict was still waging war within Moses. Who would he live for? Would he live for God or himself?

I was confronted with a similar decision during my senior year in college. Over the course of my college years, I had given up a basketball scholarship to pursue my calling in ministry. However, my brother Jared was enrolling as a freshman and had just broken

all the basketball scoring records at Selma High School in Selma, California. Having scored over a 1,000 points in his high school career, he was a hot commodity and especially at Fresno Pacific University where we were attending.

One afternoon, I heard a knock at the door of my dorm room, and when I opened the door, I was face to face with the basketball coach. He began to communicate his intention to start Jared and me as the starting guards if we would play on his team. Candidly, at that moment, I was confronted with the same question that Moses was confronted by, "Who are you living for?" My love of the game of basketball and my own personal agenda began to compete with God's plans for my life. Thankfully, I made the right choice.

However, Moses still needed some convincing, and God had to remind him of his real audience: *"I will certainly be with you. ... When you have brought the people out of Egypt, you shall serve God on this mountain"* (Exod. 3:12). In other words, "Moses, you are not the audience here; I am." However, Moses still didn't seem to get it, because he turned the focus from himself to the people.

> *Indeed, when I come to the children of Israel and say to them, "The God of your fathers has sent me to you" ... what shall I say to them?* (Exodus 3:13).

So, God once again reiterates the main issue: *"I AM who I AM ...I AM has sent me to you"* (Exod. 3:14). Are you beginning to get the picture? Moses was still living for the wrong audience when the right audience was speaking directly to him.

When Jesus walked the earth, He certainly proved His commitment to living for an audience of One. How do you think He was able to endure the agony of the Cross, the mocking and jeering of the crowds, the whippings and beatings by the Romans, the crown of thorns on His brow, the spikes in His hands and feet, the tears of His own mother, the disappointment of His disciples, and the anguish of those who had put their trust in Him? Jesus was able

to endure all of that because in a dark, lonely garden one night He made a commitment to live for an audience of One. He told His Father, *"not what I will, but what You will"* (Mark 14:36).

How were the apostles able to face such gruesome deaths for their faith? James, John's brother, was beheaded. Thomas was killed in India. Simon, the brother of James the younger, was crucified in Egypt. Simon the Zealot was crucified. Mark was burned and buried. Bartholomew was beaten, crucified, and beheaded in Armenia. Andrew was crucified in Ethiopia. Matthew was killed with a spear. Philip was stoned and crucified in Phrygia. James, the Lord's brother, died praying as a fuller smashed his skull. Peter was crucified upside down.[1] The apostles were willing to live and die for an audience of One.

Why were first-century Christians willing to be torn apart by lions, tossed on the horns of bulls, dragged through the streets with chariots, and dropped into the sea with millstones around their necks? How were they able to endure plates of hot iron on their skin, suffer through boiling oil, and allow themselves to be dipped in tar and set on fire to light up the emperor's favorite garden? They had made a decision to live for an audience of One.

Making this decision will cause you to serve Christ in life or death, in joy or sorrow, and with the cheers or the jeers. Your personal agendas will become secondary. You will minimize all other selfish gain. The prestige and power of Pharaoh's family won't overwhelm you. Your entire perspective will change. You will seek to love as God loves, see as God sees, feel as God feels, and serve as God serves.

WHO ARE YOU SEEKING TO PLEASE?

This second question is inherently interwoven with the first. Who are you seeking to please? The apostle Paul gave a very clear answer:

For do I now persuade men, or God? Or do I seek to please men? For if I still pleased men, I would not be a bondservant of Christ (Galatians 1:10).

Now some Christians will use Paul's words as a battering ram to diminish all aspects of accountability. They will exhibit a sectarian mindset that disavows any kind of submission to leadership, peers, or family, and they will ignore such Scriptures as:

Where there is no counsel, the people fall; but in the multitude of counselors there is safety (Proverbs 11:14).

Submitting to one another in the fear of God (Ephesians 5:21).

Obey those who rule over you, and be submissive, for they watch out for your souls, as those who must give an account... (Hebrews 13:17).

Serving with submission and accountability should not displace our primary commitment to please God.

Listen to the words of the apostle Paul from Galatians 1:10 again, but from a contemporary English version of the Bible:

Do you think I speak this strongly in order to manipulate crowds? Or curry favor with God? Or get popular applause? If my goal was popularity, I wouldn't bother being Christ's slave (Galatians 1:10 MSG).

When you live to gain popular applause, the trap that will ensnare you will be comparing yourself to others, and when you play the comparison game, you always lose. Comparing yourself with someone who is doing more than you are doing can easily become discouraging and disparaging. Conversely, comparing yourself with someone who is doing less than you are doing can easily cause you to become proud and arrogant. When you play the comparison game, the jeers and the cheers can cause you to stumble.

Listening to the jeers of others can cause you to struggle with maintaining a positive attitude in your service to God. On the other hand, listening to the cheers of others can cause you to struggle with a humble attitude in your service to God.

As a teenage boy, I began to preach in churches quite often. In those earlier years I didn't know any better, but the response of the crowd was extremely important to me. I would gauge the effectiveness of a sermon by the affirmation I received from others. However, after a short time I realized that the important issue was not how many people cheered but how many people changed.

Someone once told Master John Bunyan that he had preached a delightful sermon. "You are too late," said Master John, "the devil told me that before I left the pulpit."[2] In his honest confession, John Bunyan was attesting to the fact that we are far too accomplished at accepting even the smallest satisfaction in our gifts and abilities.

Unfortunately, the affirmation of people can change frequently. Jesus is the prime example of this. He heard the cheers of the crowd when He came riding into Jerusalem during His triumphant entry, but in a couple of days, those same cheers had turned to jeers as the mob began to cry, *"Crucify Him!"* (Mark 15:13).

PLEASING GOD IN THE WILDERNESS

Moses also experienced the whimsical idiosyncrasies of the crowd. The cheers of deliverance from Egypt and the Red Sea turned into jeers when he led the children of Israel into the wilderness, and they began to say:

> *"Oh, that we were back in Egypt," they moaned, "and that the Lord had killed us there! For there we had plenty*

to eat. But now you have brought us into this wilderness to kill us with starvation" (Exodus 16:3 TLB).

Moses was trying to teach a multitude of slaves who had been without spiritual leadership for 400 years to please God. As you know, he had a mountain to climb because the people were not about to give God or Moses any breaks. The only thing on their minds was satisfying their own hunger.

Some of the most difficult people to please are the ones who are only hungry to please themselves. When a spouse is only concerned about pleasing himself, you will never please him. When your boss is only concerned about pleasing herself, you will never please her. When you are only concerned about pleasing yourself, you will never please yourself. You will never get out of the wilderness until you learn to please God.

Thankfully, God didn't give up on His people because Moses said, *"And in the morning you shall see the glory of the Lord; for He hears your complaints against the Lord..."* (Exod. 16:7). God was merciful and provided for their physical hunger, and yet the people continued on to Rephidim.

PLEASING GOD IN REPHIDIM

Whereas the wilderness symbolizes a place of unsatisfied hunger, Rephidim symbolizes a place of spiritual thirst. More than likely, most Christians will end up in Rephidim at some point. Because there is no water there, they will dry up and begin to lose their hope in God.

The people began to murmur against Moses and say, *"Why is it you have brought us up out of Egypt, to kill us and our children and our livestock with thirst?"* (Exod. 17:3). The people were thirsty, and nothing but an encounter with God would satisfy their thirst.

Moses had already learned this. He had grown up playing the "acceptance game," seeking to be accepted by Pharaoh's house and his Jewish family. In the process, he became addicted to the thirst of acceptance until that addiction landed him in the desert. Only God showing up at the burning bush satisfied his thirst for acceptance and helped him fulfill his destiny.

How could Moses lead his family and the Israelites to a burning bush encounter with God if he had never been there himself? Serving others is often dependent upon your own experiences. How can you teach faith if you don't walk in faith? How can you teach giving if you are stingy? How can you teach sowing and reaping if you don't sow anything?

I have a wonderful friend who is a musician and poet. As a youth minister, Jeff Leslie experienced a devastating accident that left him as a paraplegic. However, over the years he has written some of the most beautiful songs and amazing poems. He has learned to serve others effectively from the experiences of his life. The places where you have been in life play such an important role in serving others.

At least Moses did the right thing in Rephidim when he turned to God and said, "What shall I do with this people?" There is nothing wrong with saying, "I don't know what to do." While you are serving others, there will be times when you just come to God as a fool saying, "God, I don't know what to do. I don't even know how I ended up here. Teach me what to say and how to serve." If you will humble yourself before Him, He will take you to another dimension of hope. God certainly did the same for Moses when He said:

> *Go on before the people, and take with you some of the elders of Israel. Also take in your hand your rod with which you struck the river, and go. Behold, I will stand before you there on the rock in Horeb; and you shall strike*

the rock, and water will come out of it, that the people may drink (Exodus 17:5-6).

Because Moses sought to please Him, God used a rod and a rock to bless him. The rod was symbolic of Moses's dependence upon God. It was the tool that Moses used to initiate the plagues in Egypt, and when the time came for deliverance, the Red Sea stood at attention as Moses raised the rod. Moses took it everywhere, and it was a constant reminder to the people that he was absolutely dependent upon God. It was symbolic of his hope in God.

Now there may be times you will say, *"Stand still, and see the salvation of the Lord"* only to run back behind a rock and ask God, *"Now what should we do?"* (Exod. 14:13). But you must have an unwavering dependence upon God.

In fact, one of the greatest gifts that you can give people as you serve them is an awareness of your dependence upon God. As a young boy I would travel with my parents and sing in church. The very first Scripture that I learned was Philippians 4:13, and I would stand on the piano bench next to my mother as a three-year-old and say in my own special, preschool English, "I can do all shings shrough Christ who shrengthens me."

Candidly, I still don't have a problem telling people how dependent I am on God and that without Him I can do nothing. When God created me, He created me incomplete! I am not like God who is a perfectly unified plurality of Father, Son, and Spirit. God created me fundamentally incomplete—one person.

That's why I need Him. That's why I need my wife. That's why I need my brothers and sisters in Christ. God created me with a relational vacuum that can only be filled with God and others.

Whereas the rod was symbolic of Moses' dependence upon God, the rock was symbolic of God's favor upon Moses. Despite all the murmuring and complaining, God was still initiating miracles. If you are pleasing God, He will initiate miracles even when people are fighting against you. You may have grown up on the wrong side of the tracks or feel like you are stumbling around in the wilderness, but if you have the rod of dependence in your hand, you will get water out of a rock. Just like Moses, God will provide resources from the most unlikely places. God will absolutely amaze you as you live to please Him.

RE-FORMATION CHALLENGE

Let's play the "what if" game for just a moment. What if the Hebrews had rallied behind Moses when he killed the Egyptian? Let's imagine that Moses had been able to lead the children of Israel out of Egypt at that moment in time and had not ended up in the desert. What if God had never showed up at the burning bush to address the issues of "who are you living for" and "who are you seeking to please"? Do you think Moses would have been the kind of man we know him to be in Scripture?

After all, Moses was such a mighty man of God that God talked to him face to face. Because of Moses, the world's greatest economy was turned over to a group of slaves. More happened through the life and ministry of Moses than just about anyone else in all of Scripture.

Could Moses have lasted for 40 years with a bunch of discontents and malcontents? Would Moses have been able to stand and speak the word of the Lord, even though he would be criticized and condemned by his wandering Hebrew brothers and sisters? Would he have been able to handle the pats on the back and the spit in the face—the cheers and the jeers? We will never know. Yet, what we do know is that Moses turned the corner from "living to please others" to "living to please God."

Recently, I heard about a pastor who served in a Muslim community in Northern Nigeria. Because he preached the message of Christ, he was beaten within an inch of his life. Even after he was warned to stop preaching or his wife and daughter would be physically violated, he continued to preach. Tragically, the Muslim jihadists followed through with their threat, compelling the preacher and his family to leave their community. Yet, after only a short reprieve, the preacher returned and gave his life for the sake of Christ in November of 2009.

When I heard of this amazing martyr, I didn't have to wonder if he had minimized his own personal agendas to live for an audience of One. In the words of C. T. Studd, "Only one life, 'twill soon be past, only what's done for Christ will last."[3]

RE-FORMATION PRAYER

Heavenly Father, I submit my personal agendas to You. I am not here to please myself; I am here to please You. I refuse to play the comparison game with others and seek for their applause. I refuse to become the son of Pharaoh's daughter—the son of prestige and power, the son of money and materialism, the son of peer pressure and social acceptance, or even the son of the Church and religion. Oh God, You are the One I will live for. You are the One I will serve. Whether I am in the wilderness or I am in the Promised Land, I will live for an audience of One! Whether I am receiving jeers or I am receiving cheers, I will live for an audience of One! Whether I am stressed or I am blessed, I will live for an audience of One! I will hold the rod of dependence in my hand, knowing that You will supply the rock of favor when necessary. I pray these things in Jesus's name, amen.

RE-FORMATION BUILDERS

Personal Evaluation

Moses provides an example of someone who learns to minimize his own agenda to serve others. When he tries to lead the first time, he is living for the wrong audience. However, when he experiences a God-encounter at a burning bush, his agenda changes and he begins to live for an audience of One. Allow the lessons learned through Moses's life to help you evaluate your own motives in serving others. Your hope is dependent on it.

1. Have you ever stopped long enough to evaluate your motives in serving others? If so, what was the result?

2. Much like Moses, have you ever had to make a decision between the sacred and the secular? If so, give the details.

3. Have you ever had a God-encounter, and what was the result?

4. With sincerity, answer the questions, "Who am I living for?" and "Who am I seeking to please?"

5. Write down what "living for an audience of One" means to you.

Group Discussion

Moses provides an example of someone who learns to minimize his own agenda to serve others. When he tries to lead the first time, he is living for the wrong audience. However, when he experiences a God-encounter at a burning bush, his agenda changes and he begins to live for an audience of One. Allow the lessons learned through Moses's life to help launch your discussion concerning evaluating the motives in serving others. Your hope is dependent on it.

1. Discuss the statement: "Live for an audience of One."

2. Discuss the importance of consistently evaluating motives in serving others.

3. How do the cheers and jeers affect serving others?

4. Discuss the importance of a having a "rod of dependence upon God" in ministry.

5. Discuss the quote by C. T. Studd at the end of the chapter: "Only one life, 'twill soon be past, only what's done for Christ will last."

ENDNOTES

1. *Foxe's Christian Martyrs of the World* (Westwood, NJ: Barbour and Company, Inc., 1885), 5-6.

2. *Spurgeon's Sermons*, Electronic Database. (Biblesoft, Inc, 1997, 2003, 2006).

3. C.T. Studd, "Only One Life, Twill Soon Be Past," Jesus to Europe, 2009, http://hockleys.org/2009/05/quote-only-one-life-twill-soon -be-past-poem/ (accessed February 5, 2011).

CHAPTER NINE

MOBILIZING THE NEXT GENERATION

❯❯ Biblical Challenge—AND THE MULE MOVED ON

❯❯ Biblical Example—ABSALOM

"Deal gently for my sake with the young man Absalom."
And all the people heard when the king gave all the captains
orders concerning Absalom (2 Samuel 18:5).

As we view the landscape of this post-Christian era, there is an indefeasible awareness that our hope depends on the success of the next generation. Where are the young Davids who are charging down the hill with a rag and a rock in hand?

In the book *The Bridge Generation*, Thom Rainer makes the observation that the next generation of American Christians in the 21st century is significantly lower than in preceding generations. Notice the statistics:

Builders (born 1927-1945)	65 percent Bible-based believers
Boomers (born 1946-1964)	35 percent Bible-based believers
Busters (born 1965-1983)	16 percent Bible-based believers
Bridgers (born 1984 or later)	4 percent Bible-based believers.[1]

According to Rainer's statistics, only 4 percent of those born from 1984 or later affirm that they are Bible-believing, church-attending Christians. As Ron Luce from Teen Mania promulgates, 71 million bridgers (33 million now in their teens) hold America's future in the palm of their hands.[2]

So how do we mobilize the next generation, passionately embrace them, and allow them to engage in the shaping of our ministries, churches, and denominations? How do we develop a gracious attitude that allows for "trial and error" and for testing their wings?

Most young men and women in the Church start with an innocent heart before God and Church leadership. Yet, when they discover cumbersome systems and unnecessary processes that don't contribute to effective ministry, they become disillusioned and poisoned before they approach notable service. The reality is that the next generation must be given the opportunity to test their own wings. If we protect them too much from falling, that same overprotection may keep them from flying.

One of the greatest confessions I made in serving others occurred when I stood behind a church pulpit as a 28-year-old pastor and admitted that I could not serve that congregation effectively without allowing myself any room for failure. If there was no room for failure, there was no room for flying.

So we are confronted with a choice for the next generation. We can get behind them and help them fly, or we can wage war against them so they don't even try. I opt for the former, because the next generation will accomplish great things for God that we won't even attempt.

When I was still a member of the next generation, I heard my father admit that he had watched me accomplish things that he thought were destined to fail. Although I enjoyed reveling in his admission at the time, the next generation will accomplish more with a rag and rock than we could ever imagine. The true test comes in how effectively we engage in the process of building relationship with them.

As we look at the life of Absalom, we are certainly confronted by his father David's lack of relationship with him. When we first become acquainted with Absalom, his sister Tamar has been raped by his brother Amnon, and Absalom is plotting Amnon's death. For two years, Absalom does not even speak to him.

Yet, where is their father, David, during this time? There is no evidence to suggest that David deals with the situation or tries to bring reconciliation between his sons whatsoever. The only reference to David concerning the situation was: *"But when King David heard of all these things, he was very angry"* (2 Sam. 13:21). However, when does anger translate into paternal compassion and connection with your children?

LET THE NEXT GENERATION CONNECT!

To everyone else, David was an amazing king. However, to Absalom, David was an absentee dad, and he allowed that disconnection to seethe in the soil of his soul. If David had allowed his sons to connect with him in a meaningful way, he might have salvaged their relationship and brought reconciliation.

He certainly would have seen the hatred brewing among his sons and would have known that something was up when Absalom requested for his brother Amnon to go along on a sheep-shearing

expedition (see 2 Sam. 13:24-26). If David had just connected with his sons, he might have prevented the murder of Amnon and the exile of Absalom.

The tragedy is that David knew how to connect with the next generation, even though he did not connect with his own sons. David had established a group of young men, some of which would become a part of his elite group of mighty men.

When two men killed King Ishbosheth of Israel and brought his head to David for approval, David was angry because they had killed a righteous man. So he *"...commanded his young men, and they executed them, cut off their hands and feet, and hanged them by the pool in Hebron..."* (2 Sam. 4:12).

At the time, David had not yet been anointed as the king of Israel, which occurred when he was approximately 30 years of age. That would make David's young men even younger than he was, possibly in their early twenties or even late teens.

We also know that David's young men traveled with him everywhere he went. In an earlier conversation with Ahimelech the priest, David was asked, "Why are you alone and no one is with you?" So David responded by saying:

> *The king has ordered me on some business, and said to me, "Do not let anyone know anything about the business on which I send you, or what I have commanded you." And I have directed my young men to such and such a place* (1 Samuel 21:2).

Of course, David was running for his life from King Saul at the time, but he had to give an excuse to Ahimelech concerning why his group of young men weren't with him. So, David must have made a conscious effort to mobilize his young men and have them by his side as armor bearers and protectors. They also must have ministered to his personal needs, much like the three mighty men who put their lives on the line by crossing into enemy territory just to bring him a cup of water.

Unfortunately, rather than making an excuse for why our young men aren't with us, some of us have to make an excuse why we don't have any young men. Where are today's leaders who will mentor some young men and women? Where are some leaders today who will invest their lives in the next generation to make a difference in the Kingdom of God? Tragically, David knew how to connect with his young men, but he didn't know how to connect with his own sons, especially his son Absalom.

LET THE NEXT GENERATION ARISE!

Even the generals of that day knew how to engage the next generation. When General Abner and General Joab came together at the pool of Gibeon, they said to one another, *"'Let the young men now arise and compete before us.' And Joab said, 'Let them arise'"* (2 Sam. 2:14). What a profound word for our time: "Let them arise."

More than ever we need the next generation to engage in the battle for our future. We must see them as more than a carpet-cleaning detail or a toilet patrol. We must involve them in more meaningful ministries than kissing the ring on our hand and ministering to our personal needs. We must intentionally move them from the service periphery to engage them in the battle.

Even King Saul with all his faults and failures had the courage to put young David on the battlefield against Goliath with meaningful consequences. David wasn't walking onto the battlefield representing himself only. He was representing the entire army of Israel and their families. King Saul was placing the destiny of an entire nation in the hands of a young man.

Listen to the response of Goliath when young David approached him on the battlefield: *"And when the Philistine looked about and saw David, he disdained him; for he was only a youth…"* (1 Samuel 17:42).

Notice the primary difference between Saul and Goliath. Saul ordained a young leader, while Goliath disdained a young leader. Saul could see a warrior, while Goliath only saw a child. Saul believed in the next generation, while Goliath believed in his systems of war.

We can talk about mobilizing the next generation until we become hoarse, but until we let them arise and engage in the battle, we have done nothing but talk. Just like Goliath, we have disdained them in our hearts and talked down to them without seeing their potential. Rather than believing in what they can accomplish, we have put more faith in our own systems of war, making new laws, and instituting new constitutions.

Here's a news flash! The next generation won't wear our heavy armor and attach themselves to the weapons of war that worked for us. They will use weapons we won't use. Yet, why should we care? They are willing to face giants that we aren't willing to face. If we truly desire spiritual re-formation in the 21st century, we must not forget what the next generation can do with a rag and a rock. Let them arise.

LET THE NEXT GENERATION LEAD THE WAY!

Unfortunately, King David did not see the immense talent his son Absalom possessed. Absalom would rise early in the morning and stand beside the way to the gate. Whenever anyone who had a lawsuit came to the king for a decision, Absalom would call to him and say, "What city are you from?" And he would respond, "Your servant is from such and such a tribe of Israel."

Absalom would say to him:

> *Look, your case is good and right; but there is no deputy of the king to hear you. ...Oh, that I were made judge in the land, and everyone who has any suit or cause would come to me; then I would give him justice* (2 Samuel 15:3-4).

While the people were distressed, Absalom preyed on their emotions until he stole their hearts.

Absalom was extremely talented and knew how to play the system, yet what an amazing gift he could have been to his father if he had been mentored. Absalom could have led the way in enhancing his father's greatness. However, Absalom had lived for two years in Jerusalem before David ever saw him face to face. Rejection and abandonment inflict deep wounds that are not easily overcome.

Absalom eventually stole the crown from his father, and the tribes of Israel (those who had been the last to crown David king some decades before) lent their support to Absalom. So, while David was fleeing for his life, Absalom marched on Jerusalem, and one of his first acts as king was to go in to his father's concubines in the sight of all of Israel.

By taking his father's concubines, Absalom was making himself totally abhorrent to his father and breaking down every possible bridge for reconciliation. Absalom was not just stealing the crown, but he was inflicting revenge upon his father. Perhaps if David had been there for his son, Absalom would have led the way with his father rather than against his father.

Recently, I was talking to a small group of next generation leaders who were expressing their heart-wrenching discouragement because their overtures for mentoring had been dismissed by their pastors and spiritual leaders. One young man asked the question, "What should I do when my spiritual father dismisses me?" All I could do was embrace this young man and let him know that he was valuable to me and the Church.

The Lord declared through the prophet Malachi:

> *Behold, I will send you Elijah the prophet before the coming of the great and dreadful day of the Lord. And he will turn the hearts of the fathers to the children, and*

> *the hearts of the children to their fathers, lest I come and*
> *strike the earth with a curse* (Malachi 4:5-6).

We are certainly in desperate need of the spirit of Elijah in our day if the hearts of the fathers are to be turned to the hearts of the children.

The young leaders went out of the city first.

Another example that illustrates the potential of allowing the next generation to lead the way is seen when King Ben-Hadad of Syria gathers all his forces together with 32 kings to destroy King Ahab. But the prophet Elijah shows up and tells King Ahab that God will give him the victory if he will send in the young leaders first (see 1 Kings 20:14).

"Then these young leaders of the provinces went out of the city with the army which followed them" (1 Kings 20:19). Who was the army following? They were following the young leaders. Who were the first ones to engage the enemy at the front lines? The young leaders were the first ones to engage the enemy.

These upstart, young leaders led the army out of the safe confines of the city and engaged the enemy on their own ground. We desperately need some young leaders to lead us out of the safe confines of the church and take back some of the enemy's ground. We need some young leaders who will do more than sing the old hymn "Hold the Fort," make quilts, and have potluck suppers.

The battle for planet Earth was never meant to be fought inside the walls of the church; the battle was intended to be fought on the enemy's ground. We have not enlisted in God's army to hold the fort, but to charge against the gates of hell. And who better to lead the way than the next generation?

The young leaders killed their enemy.

King Ahab sent 232 young leaders into battle, and the result was 232 victories: *"And each one killed his man; so the Syrians fled, and Israel pursued them…"* (1 Kings 20:20). What an amazing testimony! Not one of the young leaders lost a battle.

General George Marshall kept a "black book" of all the soldiers who showed promise in battle. Whenever he encountered a young soldier who demonstrated leadership ability, he added his name to the book. When a vacancy was presented in the officer corps, he would then refer to his list of qualified candidates. This system enabled Marshall to develop a large military organization filled with talented and effective officers.[3] When we mobilize young leaders, the overall quality of service will increase significantly.

LET THE NEXT GENERATION ESTABLISH ACCOUNTABILITY!

No doubt Absalom thought he would be successful in battle also. Yet, as the battle extended across the countryside, Absalom ended up in a precarious position:

> *Absalom rode on a mule. The mule went under the thick boughs of a great terebinth tree, and his head caught in the terebinth; so he was left hanging between heaven and earth. And the mule which was under him went on* (2 Samuel 18:9).

David didn't need a sword to defeat Absalom; he simply needed the branch of a tree. How much of Absalom's heavy head of hair contributed to this accident isn't recorded, but it's ironic that the very thing he was so proud of turned out to contribute to his death. Indeed, pride does lead to judgment.

Pride, pretension, and hypocrisy are the very attributes that the next generation will not tolerate. Absalom was a pretender and not a contender, and when the next generation saw it, they struck him down: *"And ten young men who bore Joab's armor surrounded Absalom, and struck and killed him"* (2 Sam. 18:15).

Where were Absalom's young men?

Yet, why was Absalom alone? We have already witnessed the fact that David and his general, Joab, had young men. But where were Absalom's young men? Absalom was wearing the crown and sitting on the throne of Israel. Where were the young men who were fighting his battles and winning his wars? Where were young men who were his armor bearers, protecting his back in moments of life or death? Joab the general had ten young men, but Absalom the king had no young men.

Tragically, the way Absalom obtained the throne was the way he ruled the kingdom. He was a "lone ranger" who stood outside the gate of Jerusalem and stole the hearts of the people. He turned the hearts of the people toward him but not the hearts of the leaders. Real leaders don't follow an Absalom to the throne; they follow a David out of town. Real leaders don't hang around position; they hang around leadership.

You always know who the godly young leaders are because they hang around other godly leaders. They follow godly leaders whether they are sitting on the throne or hiding in a cave. They follow godly leaders whether they are wearing the crown or giving the crown away. Wherever you find godly leaders, you will find other leaders, especially young leaders.

If Absalom had mobilized a generation of young leaders, they would have been there to help him out of the terebinth tree. They would have fought to the death on his behalf. Where were Absalom's young leaders? He didn't have any, and because of it, he died!

Who killed Absalom?

Isn't it ironic that Absalom was killed by the very ones he didn't have? He didn't have any young leaders, but it was Joab's young leaders who killed him. Some people seem to be concerned about keeping Absalom accountable; yet, the next generation is already committed to striking Absalom down. Because of their hatred of church politics, young leaders don't allow Absalom to last on the throne. In the grand scheme of God's design, Absalom gets what he deserves because the next generation is always there to enforce authentic spiritual re-formation.

What killed Absalom?

The young men may have struck Absalom, but it was the blatant disobedience of General Joab that ultimately killed him. The soldiers who encountered Absalom hanging from the tree didn't dare touch him. In fact, after the eyewitness who found Absalom had reported it, Joab said:

> *"You just saw him! And why did you not strike him there to the ground? I would have given you ten shekels of silver and a belt." But the man said to Joab, "Though I were to receive a thousand shekels of silver in my hand, I would not raise my hand against the king's son. For in our hearing the king commanded you and Abishai and Ittai, saying, 'Beware lest anyone touch the young man Absalom'"* (2 Samuel 18:11-12).

Joab had his own agenda. It was Joab who had orchestrated the reconciliation of David and Absalom, and now it was Joab who would get his revenge. How easy is it for the current Joab generation of leaders to have their own agendas concerning the next generation.

The Joab generation sustained many years of tremendous hardship—World War I and II, the Vietnam Crisis, the Cold War, etc. Because of these hardships, some of them have developed a "can't do it" mindset. The next generation says, "God gave me a dream." The Joab generation says, "You can't do it." The next generation says, "Someday I will lead a church of 5,000 people." The Joab generation says, "You can't do it." The next generation says, "Someday I'll touch millions." The Joab generation says, "You can't do it." What is killing the next generation is a "can't do it" mindset.

If we don't see a change in the mindset of the Joab generation, the percentage of Bible-believing, church-attending Christians in the following generation will be lower than 4 percent.
We'll lose the Davids who are destined to sit on the throne and
rule the kingdom. We'll lose the Josephs who are called to serve as
second in command for the deliverance of a nation. We'll lose the
Esthers who have the courage to challenge the status quo to save
her people. We'll lose a generation of young men and women who
will be bold in their relationship with God and who will fight for
spiritual re-formation.

RE-FORMATION CHALLENGE

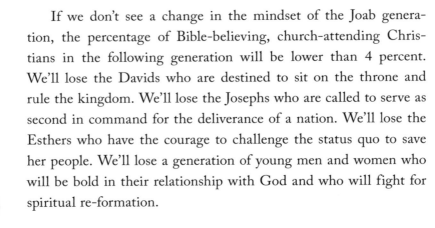

Now, notice what King David said concerning his son: *"Deal
gently for my sake with the young man Absalom"* (2 Sam. 18:5). Even
after all that Absalom had done to steal his father's throne and take
his crown, David still maintained a modicum of gentleness toward
him. Unfortunately, today we see very little patience and tolerance
for the next generation at times. Minds are made up, and judgment
is meted out without the proper gentleness to accompany it.

One may say, "But we don't want any young Absaloms; we
want some young Davids." How are young Davids formed if they
don't have godly fathers and mothers to help raise them? Why do
you think Saul had no giant-killers in his army, and David had five
giant killers in his army? Saul wasn't a giant-killer and didn't mobilize any giant-killers, while David was a giant-killer and mobilized
five others.

The sad part of this account is found after Absalom is caught
in the tree. He is hanging suspended between heaven and earth,
and he is still alive. Yet, there is a small phrase that brings finality
to the situation: *"And the mule which was under him went on"* (2 Sam.
18:9). There was still an opportunity for Absalom's rescue, but even
the mule moved on.

There is sorrow and sadness in the existence of a ministry, church, or denomination that doesn't recognize the need to return for their young men and women. The old mule doesn't even wait around long enough to see what will become of them. She may be carrying a young Absalom, or maybe, just maybe, a young David. Yet, she will never know.

When you have served for an extended period of time, sometimes you can develop a "service-as-usual" mindset and never look back long enough to see that you may have been the one who left that young man or young woman hanging in the terebinth tree. Their hair was caught in a mess of a problem; and yet, you never turned back to see what would become of them or whether you could have made a difference. *And the mule moved on!*

What is the terebinth tree known for anyway? Its shade. It was short and broad, and if you needed shade, you went to the terebinth tree. Unfortunately, the next generation is finding the terebinth tree, but they are not finding shade. Instead, they are hanging themselves with all kinds of man-made systems and structures that are not life-giving. The Joab generation is disregarding the words of the king: *"Deal gently for my sake with the young man Absalom."* So the epitaph on Absalom's tombstone reads: *And the mule moved on!*

At one time Absalom was the most popular man in the kingdom. He was an up-and-coming, next-generation leader, but now he is buried in a pit and his body is covered with stones. Apparently, Absalom's three sons have died also, so there is no one left in his family to perpetuate his name. How did this end up happening? *And the mule moved on!*

In April of 2010, I was privileged to attend the Empower 21 Conference on the campus of Oral Roberts University. The conference was focused toward empowering 21st-century Christians with a fresh revival of Pentecost. During one of the worship gatherings, ten ORU students were asked the question, "How should we pray

for your generation?" They responded by sharing that we should pray for the following:

1. That spiritual fathers and mothers would step up

2. That they would find their identity as sons and daughters of God

3. That they would focus in the midst of a distracting culture

4. That they would receive revelation knowledge and communication from the fathers

5. That they would hear the voice of God without it being tainted by what they want to hear

6. That they would stand before the Lord in purity

7. That they would have relentless love for the lost

8. That they would be righteous examples of Christ

9. That they would have roots of purity

10. That they would provide biblical education to the nations

With young, discerning leaders like these students, we have hope, a bright future, and an opportunity to see spiritual re-formation impact the world.

Perhaps we should remember the age of David when he began ruling in Israel, the age of Joseph when he was second in command to Pharaoh, and the age of Jesus when he was at the zenith of His public ministry. Three of the greatest leaders of Scripture were in their early 30s! For spiritual re-formation to occur, we must partner together to mobilize the next generation in Christian service.

RE-FORMATION PRAYER

Heavenly Father, forgive me for my lack of connection with the next generation. Forgive me for becoming an absentee parent. Forgive me for allowing the next generation to hang in a tree of their own demise while I move on with Christian service as usual. Please help me to push past my own discomfort and engage them in the battle for our future. May we not lose another generation to the destruction of the enemy! May we not lose another generation to the pain of rejection and abandonment! May we not lose another generation because we coerced them into wearing our own armor! Let them arise! Let them lead the way! Let them be victorious over the enemy of their souls in Jesus's name, amen.

RE-FORMATION BUILDERS

Personal Evaluation

Absalom provides an example of what happens when the next generation is left hanging without spiritual fathers and mothers. One would wonder if Absalom's life could have turned out differently if his father had provided the necessary support system. Allow the lessons learned through the life of Absalom to help you evaluate your responsibility to the next generation.

1. Absalom struggled with an absentee father. Can you relate to this, and if so, how?

2. Identify and list the young leaders whom God has placed in your life.

3. How can you build a deeper relationship with young leaders in your life?

4. How can you protect the next generation from the Joab generation who seeks to harm them by restricting their dreams?

5. What does the phrase "and the mule moved on" mean to you?

Group Discussion

Absalom provides an example of what happens when the next generation is left hanging without spiritual fathers and mothers. One would wonder if Absalom's life could have turned out differently if his father had provided the necessary support system. Allow the lessons learned through the life of Absalom to help you evaluate your responsibility to the next generation.

1. According to Rainer's statistics, only 4 percent of those born from 1984 or later affirm that they are Bible-believing, church-attending Christians. Discuss the reasons for the declining faith in the next generation.

2. As Ron Luce from Teen Mania promulgates, 71 million bridgers (33 million now in their teens) hold America's future in the palm of their hands. How does this heighten the importance of mobilizing the next generation?

3. David's lack of involvement in the life of Absalom affected his decisions and actions. Discuss how the

current phenomenon of absentee fathers is affecting the next generation.

4. Absalom was extremely talented, according to Scripture. What are some ways that the Church can capitalize on the next generation's gifts and talents?

5. Discuss ways that the next generation can be protected from the Joab generation who seeks to do them harm by restricting their dreams.

6. What does the phrase "and the mule moved on" mean to you?

7. This would be a good time to pray over the prayer requests provided by the ORU students for their generation:

> That spiritual fathers and mothers would step up
>
> That they would find their identity as sons and daughters of God
>
> That they would focus in the midst of a distracting culture
>
> That they would receive revelation knowledge and communication from the fathers
>
> That they would hear the voice of God without it being tainted by what they want to hear
>
> That they would stand before the Lord in purity
>
> That they would have relentless love for the lost
>
> That they would be righteous examples of Christ
>
> That they would have roots of purity
>
> That they would provide biblical education to the nations

ENDNOTES

1. Thom S. Rainer, *The Bridge Generation: America's Second Largest Generation, What They Believe, How to Reach Them* (Nashville, TN: Broadman and Holman Publishers, 1997).

2. Ron Luce, *Battle Cry for a Generation* (Colorado Springs, CO: Cook Communications Ministries, 2005), 31.

3. Henry Blackaby and Richard Blackaby, *Spiritual Leadership* (Nashville, TN: Broadman and Holman Publishers, 2001), 135.

THE VIOLENT TAKE IT BY FORCE!

The world is changed;
I feel it in the water;
I feel it in the earth;
I smell it in the air;
Much that once was, is lost,
For none now live who remember it.[1]

These are the words of Galadriel at the beginning of *The Fellowship of the Ring*, the first movie in the *Lord of the Rings* trilogy. At the opening of the story, life for Tolkien's elves, dwarves, men, and hobbits is growing bleak and dark as a metamorphosis begins to shape Middle Earth. In much the same way, our world seems to be moving down a path of extraordinary change. You can feel it in the atmosphere, and you can smell it in the air around you. The battle between light and darkness is intensifying.

In his book, *The American Church in Crisis,* David T. Olsen observed that 52 million Americans—17.5 percent of the American

population—attended church on any given weekend in 2005. He also observed that no single state saw church attendance keep up with the population growth.[2] Declining church attendance is a red flag for declining spiritual sensitivity in America.

Lou Allison, who was connected with the Billy Graham Center for Evangelism, spoke accurately when he said, "The distance between pre-Christians and faith in Christ is a much longer distance than it was in previous generations."[3]

If America, indeed, is becoming a post-Christian nation, then the prayer and proclamation for spiritual re-formation must become more forceful and aggressive. Christians who are truly re-formed in Christ must be willing to pass their experience on, leading others through the same grand adventure.

When I was in college in the mid-'80s, we used to watch these powder-puff football games. Some of the college girls would come out wearing these big red flags around their waist. The girls didn't have to tackle each other. All they needed to do was grab the red flag.

Pardon my lack of enthusiasm, but I can remember when the Kansas City Chiefs had a middle linebacker by the name of Mike "Mad Dog" Maslowsky who would have never understood pulling a flag. In one particular game, he had a concussion or some kind of head injury, so some of the coaches hid his helmet, trying to keep him from sneaking back into the game. Now that's football!

Unfortunately, we are trying to play flag football in a complacent Christian culture where the enemy of the Church is gaining ground. We are acting like the battle for earth is merely a game, telling the devil, "You can pull my big red flag, but you can't tackle me." While we are worried about getting our uniforms dirty, he is laughing at us and taking out our spouses, children, bosses, and neighbors. We have exchanged "biblical Christianity" for "powder-puff Christianity," and we have become an easy mark for the devil.

Fortunately, we can turn the tide of destruction by leading the charge in spiritual re-formation. Now, I realize that someone might say, "Aren't Christians called to turn the other cheek or play the role of the peacemaker? Isn't the Church all about loving your enemy and going the extra mile?" Spiritual re-formation doesn't seem to resonate with turning-the-other-cheek theology and going-the-extra-mile ministry.

However, perhaps we should consider another perspective in Scripture. One of the most forceful chapters in the Old Testament is found in Joshua 6. It's an action chapter or "just do it" chapter. The strategic planning is over. The supply camp pampering is a thing of the past. The fear factor hurdle has been successfully jumped. The people are now marching around the walls of Jericho and shouting to declare the arrival of God. Let's consider what happens:

> *So the people shouted when the priests blew the trumpets. And it happened when the people heard the sound of the trumpet, and the people shouted with a great shout, that the wall fell down flat. Then the people went up into the city, every man straight before him, and they took the city. And they utterly destroyed all that was in the city, both man and woman, young and old, ox and sheep and donkey, with the edge of the sword* (Joshua 6:20-21).

This event sounds violent. Destroying a city and murdering men, women, and animals with a sword sounds messy. But then, taking the enemy's territory is violent and messy! Just ask Jesus when He died on the Cross to destroy the works of the devil. Biblical evidence seems to suggest that there was a violent and messy side of Jesus.

FORCEFUL SIDE OF JESUS

Perhaps, the Church of the living Lord has forgotten to preach one entire side of Jesus. We often hear of the meek Jesus who:

- Said, *"Love your enemies, bless those who curse you"* (Matt. 5:44).

- Did not have a place to lay His head (see Matt. 8:20).

- Said, *"All who take up the sword will perish by the sword"* (Matt. 26:52).

- Did not answer Pilate with a single word (see Matt. 27:14).

- Turned His cheek to the Roman soldiers (see Matt. 27:30).

- Suffered unmercifully down the Via Dolorosa.

- Could have called down 12 legions of angels, but didn't do so.

So, we often hear of the meek Jesus, but we don't hear of the forceful Jesus who:

- Rebuked the Pharisees and called them white-washed tombs (see Matt. 23:27).

- Remained in the Temple and eventually told His parents that He needed to be about the Father's business (see Luke 2:49).

- Commanded the storm and sea to be still (see Mark 4:39).

- Demanded satan to leave by saying, *"Away with you, Satan!"* (Matt. 4:10).

- Rebuked Peter by saying, *"Get behind me, Satan!"* (Matt. 16:23).

- Cast out the money changers and all those who sold doves (see Mark 11:15).

Jesus was forceful, and He used forceful terminology in such passages of Scripture as:

> *And when He had called* [Greek *diatasso*: ordered or charged] *His twelve disciples to Him, He gave them power over unclean spirits, to cast them out, and to heal all kinds of sickness and all kinds of disease* (Matthew 10:1).

> *And as you go, preach, saying, "The kingdom of heaven is at hand." Heal the sick, cleanse the lepers, raise the dead, cast out demons. Freely you have received, freely give* (Matthew 10:7-8).

> *Do not think that I came to bring peace on the earth. I did not come to bring peace but a sword. For I have come to "set a man against his father, a daughter against her mother, and a daughter-in-law against her mother-in-law"; and "a man's enemies will be those of his own household." He who loves father or mother more than Me is not worthy of Me. And he who loves son or daughter more than Me is not worthy of Me* (Matthew 10:34-37).

Are you beginning to get the picture? Perhaps spiritual re-formation is dependent upon our willingness to follow the forceful side of Jesus.

FORCEFUL SIDE OF THE CHRISTIAN

Charles Finney once declared:

> I pray you let us probe the consciences of our hearers; let us thunder forth the law and the Gospel of God

until our voices reach the capital of this nation. ...If immorality prevails in the land, the fault is ours in a great degree. If there is a decay of conscience, the pulpit is responsible for it. Let us not ignore this fact my dear brethren, but let us lay it to heart and be thoroughly awake to our responsibility in respect to the morals of this nation.[4]

John the Baptist was certainly one who exemplified this kind of approach to spiritual re-formation. What was John the Baptist known for? He was known for his wild and forceful side. This guy was still wearing Old Testament garb—garments made of camel's hair and a leather belt! Some of us may be a few years behind the times in our apparel; John the Baptist was 1,000 years behind the times. He was still wearing what the Old Testament prophets wore and eating bugs and wild honey.

Yet, John was filled with the Holy Spirit while he was still in his mother's womb, and when he faced the self-appointed righteous, he looked them in the eye and called them a *"brood of vipers"* (Luke 3:7). He even pointed his finger in King Herod's face and called him an adulterer (see John 3:19). He eventually lost his head for that one, but he was forceful!

In Matthew 11, Jesus began to say to the multitudes concerning John, *"What did you go out into the wilderness to see? A reed shaken by the wind?"* (Matt. 11:7). Down by the banks of the Jordan River, the long reeds of grass grew readily and freely. The phrase "a shaken reed" was a common sight. In other words, Jesus was saying, "What did you go out into the wilderness to see? An ordinary reed (man) shaken in the wind? Did you go out to see a weak vacillating reed?"

Jesus went on to say to the multitude:

But what did you go out to see? A man clothed in soft garments? Indeed, those who wear soft clothing are in kings' houses (Matthew 11:8).

Soft (Greek: *malakos*) means "soft to the touch."[5] Did you go out to see a softy or a "do nothin' do gooder" that has no moxy? Softies are reserved for the king's house, where they don't miss too many chicken dinners. They're pampered and babied and well-fed, and they camp out on the couch with no courage!

But what did you go out to see? A prophet? Yes, I say to you, and more than a prophet. For this is he of whom it is written: "Behold, I send My messenger before Your face, who will prepare Your way before You" (Matthew 11:9).

Jesus was stating the obvious: "You didn't go out to see just another prophet or representative of God. You didn't go out to see just another man make a speech. You went out to see My messenger. He is not a reed shaken with the wind, a weak vacillator, or a softy pampered and babied man in a king's house! He is a re-formation man—a 'preparer of the way' man!" In fact, Jesus's testimony of John was absolutely amazing:

Assuredly, I say to you, among those born of women there has not risen one greater than John the Baptist; but he who is least in the kingdom of heaven is greater than he (Matthew 11:11).

In other words, John walked in a measure of spiritual authority that was greater than all other people during his time. However, after Jesus's death, resurrection, and ascension, the forceful nature of the Kingdom was offered to every Christian in a greater dimension than was afforded to John.

That greater dimension became Luke 17:21: "...*the kingdom of God is within you.*" Every Christian became a living representative

RE◊FORMING A NEW YOU

of the Kingdom of God. Literally, you became the Kingdom! Whatever happens to the Kingdom happens to you. That's why Christ continues to say:

> And from the days of John the Baptist until now the kingdom of heaven suffers violence, and the violent take it by force (Matthew 11:12).

If you are suffering violence, the Kingdom of Heaven is suffering violence. To overcome, you must become a member of the "violent." Now, you might be saying, "I don't want to be numbered with the violent." But the meaning of the word *violent* is to be "forceful" (Greek: *biastai*).[6] So, Jesus was simply declaring that the Kingdom of Heaven is suffering a forceful invasion from the forces of darkness, and those who overcome will be the violent or forceful ones. This is certainly a different perspective for those who only advocate a "turn the other cheek" theology.

RE-FORMATION CHALLENGE

One of my favorite books in the New Testament is Ephesians. It's called the "queen" of Paul's letters! After the apostle Paul gives such wonderful instruction in the practical areas of life—marriage, family, parenting, and service in the church—he summarizes by saying:

> In conclusion, be strong in the Lord [be empowered through your union with Him]; draw your strength from Him [that strength which His boundless might provides] (Ephesians 6:10 AMP).

The entire book is summarized with the words, "Be strong in the Lord." This is one of those "darts to the heart" or one of those biblical truths that calls us to spiritual re-formation. In other words, if you want to see re-formation in your life, your marriage and family, and your service to God, you must be strong or forceful in the Lord.

The words of the psalmist also echo this when he said, *"Blessed be the Lord my Rock, who trains my hands for war, and my fingers for battle"* (Ps. 144:1). Here is an important question for you to consider, "Are your hands trained for war and your fingers ready for battle?"

One afternoon, I was sitting in the dentist's office awaiting my dreadful time in the dental chair when I overheard three ladies talking about their Sunday-morning church experiences. One of the ladies said, "My church always has a greeting time where we are expected to walk around and shake hands with people. This past Sunday I didn't shake anyone's hand. You don't know what kind of bacteria you can pick up from people." The other two ladies agreed, and the conversation continued for the next several minutes.

Finally, the spiritual re-former in me couldn't keep quiet any longer. I stood up, walked over to them, and said, "Ladies, I couldn't help overhearing your conversation concerning keeping your hands clean. My wife and I would like to invite you to come along with us on a missions trip to Africa. There are lots of people who need to know Christ. But here will be the challenge for you. You will have to get your hands dirty." As you can imagine, those wonderful ladies didn't have much to say. The truth is that if you are not willing to touch people in the church, you probably won't touch people outside the church.

Hands that are trained for war and fingers that are ready for battle will get dirty. The spiritually unresolved or non-Christians in our world are not looking for the "clean hands people." They are not looking for "fair-weather Christians" who only serve Christ as long as the sky is blue, and they are certainly not looking for chicken-dinner churchites who do not want to touch you because you may have bacteria.

Re-formation is defined as "forming a new person, removing the defects for a better way of life, and improving all systems for

transformation."[7] My hope is that you are well on your way to experiencing a new *you* through the life re-forming guidance of God and that Christ has connected to every area in your life, transforming you and the culture around you.

According to the words of Galadriel in *The Fellowship of the Ring*, "The world is changed."[8] The challenge of spiritual reformation is how we now respond to that change. We can succumb to the words of Matthew Arnold:

> The sea of Faith
> Was once, too, at the full, and round earth's shore
> Lay like the folds of a bright girdle furled.
> But now I only hear
> Its melancholy, long, withdrawing roar.[9]

Or we can abide by the pledge of the French Foreign Legion: "If I falter, push me on; if I stumble, pick me up; if I retreat, shoot me."[10]

The *tension* of spiritual re-formation involves freely living in the midst of spiritual dissonance without any contemplation of retreat. The *test* of spiritual re-formation includes submitting to the process of allowing your heavenly Father to take the pieces of your life apart and put them back together again. The *triumph* of spiritual re-formation involves becoming a tangible presence of transformation to the world.

To reiterate what Charles Finney declared: "I pray you let us probe the consciences of our hearers; let us thunder forth the law and the Gospel of God until our voices reach the capital of this nation...."[11]

RE-FORMATION PRAYER

Heavenly Father, the Kingdom of Heaven is suffering violence! Bodies are being ravaged with sickness! Children are starving from neglect! Homes are being destroyed by sin! Raise my spiritual sensitivity! Teach my hands to war and my fingers to fight! Teach me to be a spiritual re-former! Greater is He who is in me than he who is in the world! Sickness and disease must bow to the Kingdom of God in me! Neglect and selfishness must bow to the Kingdom of God in me! Division and destruction must bow to the Kingdom of God in me! In Jesus's name, amen!

ENDNOTES

1. J. R. R. Tolkien, *The Fellowship of the Ring* (New York: Houghton Mifflin, 2002), 772.

2. David T. Olsen, *The American Church in Crisis* (Grand Rapids, MI: Zondervan, 2008), 36-37.

3. Tom Wright, *Paul for Everyone: Romans, part 1* (Louisville, KY: Westminster John Knox, 2004), 11-12.

4. Charles Finney, "The Seared Conscience," *The Oberlin Evangelist*, 1965.

5. James Strong, *Biblesoft's New Exhaustive Strong's Numbers and Concordance with Expanded Greek-Hebrew Dictionary*, (Seattle, WA: Biblesoft, Inc., 1994, 2003, 2006).

6. *Ibid.*

7. *Webster's Dictionary*, s.v. "Re-formation."

8. Tolkien, *The Fellowship of the Ring*, 772.

9. Matthew Arnold, "Dover Beach," in New Poems (London: Macmillan, 1876).

10. James S. Hewett, *Illustrations Unlimited* (Wheaton, IL: Tyndale House Publishers, Inc., 1988), 128.

11. Finney, "The Seared Conscience."

ABOUT WAYMAN MING, JR.

As a gifted leader, teacher, and musician, Wayman Ming Jr. has traveled to over 30 nations of the world calling for spiritual re-formation. His resume of ministry includes serving on faculty at Messenger College in Joplin, Missouri for five years; serving as lead pastor of Joplin Family Worship Center in Joplin, Missouri, for 11 years; serving as founder and president of Harvest Impact Ministries since 2000; and serving as the General Secretary of the Pentecostal Church of God. With a dream for 21st-century re-formation, he delivers a passionate plea for Christian relevance and declares a challenging and life-changing message.

IN THE RIGHT HANDS, THIS BOOK WILL CHANGE LIVES!

Most of the people who need this message will not be looking for this book. To change their lives, you need to put a copy of this book in their hands.

> *But others (seeds) fell into good ground, and brought forth fruit, some a hundred-fold, some sixty-fold, some thirty-fold* (Matthew 13:8).

Our ministry is constantly seeking methods to find the good ground, the people who need this anointed message to change their lives. Will you help us reach these people?

> *Remember this—a farmer who plants only a few seeds will get a small crop. But the one who plants generously will get a generous crop* (2 Corinthians 9:6).

**EXTEND THIS MINISTRY BY SOWING
3 BOOKS, 5 BOOKS, 10 BOOKS, OR MORE TODAY,
AND BECOME A LIFE CHANGER!**

Thank you,

Don Nori Sr., Founder
Destiny Image
Since 1982